Just *Joan*

JOAN POPE HERNDON

authorHOUSE®

AuthorHouse™
1663 Liberty Drive
Bloomington, IN 47403
www.authorhouse.com
Phone: 833-262-8899

Published by AuthorHouse 08/26/2020

ISBN: 978-1-7283-7024-8 (sc)
ISBN: 978-1-7283-7023-1 (e)

Print information available on the last page.

DEDICATION

I dedicate this book to my best friend Wanda Green, better known as Wendy. There is so much I can say about Wendy. Good and positive things. When I wrote this book Wendy was with us, but since I wrote this dedication Wendy has passed away from illness. There is no better way to express my feelings about Wendy except through this song, and I quote:

To Sir With Love
By Lulu
"Those schoolgirl days of telling tales
And biting nails are gone
But in my mind I know
They will still live on and on

But how do you thank someone
Who has taken you from crayons to perfume?
It isn't easy, but I'll try"

PRELUDE

This is my second book I started. My first book I started in the fifth grade. I realized I did not know much about life so I quit writing the book. You'll find this book which was in me, because ten days to write, this book is very honest and to the point. No offense to anyone.

First of all I like to mention my deceased father who knew nothing about this book. He raised ten children with Ma. He was a very raw person in his personality. Without his rawness I wouldn't have the quality of being raw myself.

My mother I would like to thank her for the compassion she had for her ten children, which made up for the rawness of my father.

My nine siblings with their unique personalities and strengths, which was very much linked to my personality, in words and deeds.

My ex-husband whom is deceased, He wrote a short story before he died, and for some reason right after his death I sat down and wrote my life story.

Last but not least I'd like to thank Jehovah God, the most important spirit person in my life. He is preserving my life up until now.

Nothing too special just the average life of the American girl next door.

Holliswood, if you could!!!!!

CHAPTER 1

As one of my siblings would say, "But Daddy, its Joan's birthday!"And Daddy would turn around and say, "YOU, YOU...You were born on the coldest day of the year. I don't know how I got your mother to the hospital."Then Ma would interrupt Daddy and tell the same story every time."There was ice everywhere, and we had to go up a hill then down a hill. It was like an ice-skating rink."Then Daddy would proudly announce, "But I got her there safe and sound," to which Ma would reply, "And you were born at ten twenty in the morning." This is what happened each year on my birthday.

Daddy would stomp down the stairs, usually in a bad mood because we were all home from school. He would demand to know why all these children were home and making so much noise. He never seemed to realize it was my birthday until someone would begin. You see I was born on Abraham Lincoln's birthday - February 12, - and in those days we didn't go to school on the actual day he was born.

I was born in the Hollis neighborhood of Queens, New York City and always thought I was special because I did not have to do any chores on my birthday. No school, no chores. Yahoo! Being born on both a national holiday and the coldest day of that year in New York City may explain why I can be twice as nice or cold as ice.

My first birthday was memorable, even for an infant like me, probably because I was shocked into the reality of the day. Like most people, I remember shocking things, even from an early age.

My family put me in a highchair in the kitchen. They placed a cupcake in front of me with a lit candle right on the top. I don't remember what kind of cupcake it was, but I do remember the lit candle. It was the fire that caught my attention. It must have put me into shock of some kind because I remember the scene so well. There were a lot of people gathering around me, singing an awful tune and then the fire. Fire was naturally shocking to me at that early age. By the way, don't worry, someone else blew the candle out.

As if fire weren't enough for a young child, I was nearly crushed one night by a sleeping parent. I was in the bed with Daddy and Ma. I must have been one years old because my sister Gail, who was fourteen months younger than me, was in the crib. Boy was she making an awful racket crying and carrying on. Momma must have gotten up to tend to her and Daddy, still mostly asleep, just rolled right over on top of me. Now that is enough to get any child's attention. Needless to say, I never slept in the same bed with them again.

You must be wondering where this story is going. Well the reason I mention the shocking things I remember from an early age is because these are the things I remember most about my early life and about my family. I'm not here to tell my family secrets or anything degrading, as a matter of fact this is going to be a clean story. The truly shocking things that happened in my family were mostly different things. Things like verbal abuse, sometimes physical abuse, and even occasional mental abuse. In today's society the kinds of activities that went on in my family would not be tolerated, but back then, these were normal everyday activities in most of the families I knew.

Now some of you may not be familiar with the phrase "clean story." Most stories today are not what I consider "clean" stories. If this story was a movie, I would probably rate my book as "PG," as oppose to "R" rated. For me, I cannot read or write an "R" rated story and don't even think about "X" rated. To me whether a story is fact or fiction, "PG" rating is innocent, or as I would call it, clean. Those other stories, I consider them unclean. Depends on subject.

That's just how I feel but to each his own. And if you haven't read a clean story lately read on. You might be ready to quit, but wait. This is America, the land of the dysfunctional American families and while it may not be pretty, we are all in it together.

Even we dysfunctionals have love, hate, humor, and truth and that is what this book is all about, so read on.

I guess you might call me a Queens girl. Anyone can tell you what that means if they are from New York City. As far as the girl next door, that was me too.

Around my family, I was considered the quiet one. I mostly didn't say much at home because I didn't have much to say. I basically watched everyone and believe me there was a lot to see, and hear, at least what they wanted me to see and hear.

Daddy and Ma had ten children together. I say together for the benefit of my California friends. You see most of the people I grew up with in New York had the same mother and father as their siblings, and these were large families. There were not very many of what might be called stepfamilies. When I moved to California just about everyone I met came from a stepfamily household. One new friend told me that when he was in school, he was the only person in his class whose mom and dad were not divorced, and this friend was the same age as me. I always had to explain to people that all my brothers and sisters had the same mom and dad, all ten of us. I never felt like I was the norm in California. That must be because I didn't come from one of those stepfamily household.

Daddy grew up in a small family, but Ma came from a big family. They were both raised in the small rural community of Whatley, Alabama. You can put the map down; you probably won't find it. When I say small, I mean really small. How small you might ask?It was so small you were as likely to be related as live in the same neighborhood. Let me demonstrate.

My grandfather on my mother's side, his name was John, was widowed in the early 1930s with a house full of children. Before Granddaddy married his first wife, my grandmother, he dated my father's Aunt, Lula. This happened before my parents were born. But he wouldn't marry my father's Aunt because she was not a tidy housekeeper. Thank God he didn't marry my fathers' Aunt for I would not be here. He married my mother's mother and had eight kids with her. Too close for comfort!Amen!

Well it seemed that Lula had plenty of charms, but housekeeping was not one of them. Granddaddy John met and married my grandmother named Cornelia. They had a daughter named Desma, who eventually became my mother. Just think, if my grandfather married Lula, who eventually became my father's Aunt, there might never have been me or my mother. So, you see that's why Whatley, Alabama is known for its close relations. Too close, if you ask me.

That story gives me a headache, and I'm the one telling it. So, let's get back to Daddy and Ma. They were married in 1946 in Fairfield, Alabama. Why Fairfield, Alabama you say? Well, when my mother's mother died my mother was nine years old. Her oldest sibling, who was her sister, was already married to man in Fairfield, Alabama. Ma went to live with her sister and her husband after the death of her mother. Ma would go back to Whatley in the summer and school holidays to stay with her father and brothers. According to Ma, she couldn't wait to return to the country, which she considered her real home. So, Ma actually grew up in two places: Whatley, Alabama and Fairfield, Alabama. Daddy and Ma's wedding was in her sister's house in Fairfield.

In 1946 Daddy and Ma left the quiet of Alabama for the lights of Harlem USA. Daddy and Ma moved in with Daddy's mother and eventually got their own two-bedroom flat of their own. We will talk about that later.

They must have been pretty happy since they soon had six children and they were all still living in that little two-bedroom flat. Can you imagine?No wonder Ma told Daddy, "If you don't get me out of here, I'm going back to my father's house in Alabama."Daddy took her threat seriously and bought a house in Queens, NYC.

Daddy loved to tell us all that when he bought that house, he signed his life away and walked away with 50 cents in his pocket, six kids to feed, but a happy wife. I guess Ma was real happy cause soon enough number seven child was on the way - me. I was born on the coldest day of the year. February 12, 1958. You remember that story, don't you?? First born in Hollis, Queens NYC.

CHAPTER 2

Before I get into writing more about me, let me tell you about Daddy and Ma. After all, I would not be here if it weren't for them.

Daddy and Ma started out married in 1946 in Fairfield, Alabama. After marriage, they immediately moved to Harlem, New York City. Like I said before, Daddy's mother was living in Harlem at the time. We kids called my grandmother Nanny. You might say that my grandmother was a somewhat peculiar person.

Nanny only had one natural child, my father. When I was a little girl, she adopted a daughter. I do not remember how old my adoptive Aunt was when Nanny adopted her, but I do know she is at least nine years older than me. I can't say too much for Nanny's parenting skills since she didn't actually raise my father, his Aunt did. That's right; my grandfather's sister raised my father. Here is how that happened.

Daddy's father was named Zachery Pope and he had a sister named Lula Pope. That made Lula my daddy's aunt. I do not know very much about Zachery Pope since he died before Daddy even went to school. Nanny found herself single and didn't want to raise a child on her own, although I will say that she did at least try. In the end, Nanny gave up Daddy to his Aunt Lula.

Ma made sure we knew all this. There were times that Nanny was in our lives and times she wasn't. But one thing I do remember is how she could get us girls laughing. Nanny was what you might call open minded about life and she was very funny at times. She would tell us about some of the "olden days," as she called them and the exciting things she did while growing up.

Nanny was a real fighter, and not just with words. She had physically fought some people, especially if there was a need to protect her younger brother. I confess I don't remember specifics about many of her stories, but I do remember how open minded she was. It was great to be able to talk to Nanny about so many things I couldn't discuss with my own mother, especially about; you know, the opposite sex, b-o-y-s. Believe me, back in the day most people did not talk to their children about the opposite sex. But Nanny would talk to me about that and almost anything. She helped me grow in that particular way.

Nanny always seemed to move a lot. This could have something to do with her having her share of husbands. Strangely, I really don't remember seeing her with a man. Maybe her husbands were some sort of early "urban legends."

Sometimes I liked being around Nanny and sometimes I didn't. Much of the time I thought she lived in boring places with not much for us to do. She lived in the Corona neighborhood of Queens. Looking back, it is funny how a young child creates opinions about places. You see, from the mid-1940s through the 1960s, Corona, and its neighbor East Elmhurst, were home to many legendary black people. This area was home to Malcolm X, Dizzy Gillespie, Ella Fitzgerald, and many more. I guess I should have paid closer attention, but I was a kid.

Now back to Ma and Daddy. Daddy had served in World War II and Ma told me that he received an Army check from the Army. Even so, the money from the government did not last long so Daddy, as a responsible married man, got his first job. This job was at a hotel in downtown New York City where he was a cook. To bring in more money, he also worked part time at the brewery in downtown New York City. The job as a cook at the hotel was his main job and the brewery was a side job. According to Ma, the brewery workers could drink all the beer they wanted. Ma thought it was a Budweiser brewery but wasn't totally sure. Whatever the brand, the extra money helped them make ends meet.

With limited income, Ma and Daddy initially lived with Nanny in a sixth-floor walkup apartment on East 164th Street, not far from the Yankee Stadium in the Bronx. Ma said it was hard to get an apartment in Harlem back then. They would tell Daddy he made too much money. Can you believe that?Ma said black people were moving in droves to New York City from the southern states, and a lot of them were getting relief, what we now call welfare. I guess people with children on relief got first pick of the apartments. At the time, Daddy and Ma had no children and Daddy made a whopping forty bucks a week. So, the superintendent in Nanny's building helped Daddy and Ma get their first apartment. The connection was that the superintendent in the Nanny's building was the Uncle to the superintendent in the building Ma and Daddy eventually moved to. Even back then, New York City was all about making connections.

Ma liked the Harlem apartment because it had two bedrooms and was on the first floor. In the 1940s, most buildings in Harlem had about six floors and no elevators. Their first address was at 15 East 118 Street and they paid monthly rent of just $23.00. Can you believe that?I don't even want to think what a two-bedroom apartment in Harlem would cost today.

Back in the forties when Daddy and Ma started out in Harlem was an exciting place to live. Ma used to tell us that her front door opened right at the street. This made it easy for Ma to spend her days at the park with her children, except for nap time of course. Mount Morris Park was the name of the park they would go to. Ma preferred the park to hanging out by her front door like most people did in Harlem.

Even though I was born in Queens, I still remember going to Harlem as a little girl and visiting some of Daddy's relatives. It was like a different world for me, like something from an earlier time. The apartments were all so old fashion. They had chains to pull for the toilets. The kitchens had deep sinks; I guess they were for bathing also. But when Daddy and Ma lived there it certainly didn't seem old fashion to them. You see in the place they were from, Whatley, Alabama, many of the homes didn't have indoor bathrooms or even electricity. In many ways I was glad I wasn't raised in Harlem, although the street life would have been very exciting.

In both Harlem and in Queens, Ma made friends quickly with the neighbors. They were some pretty colorful characters, and by that, I mean they were fun and interesting. Most of Ma's friends were from the southern states, so there was a certain kinship.

It was a very interesting time for people of color back then. Although my parents were not famous, somehow, I think they should have made the history books. We all contributed to creating the society we know today. One story that my mother told me is about her name, Desma.

When Ma had her first baby at Manhattan Hospital, the nurse gave her a book of suggested baby names. Well when Ma came back to the same hospital a year later to have her second baby, they gave her a different baby book. To her surprise, her own name, Desma, had been added to the book. One year later and there was my mother's name, right in the book of baby names. To me, that makes my mother sort of famous.

When I think of the 1940s in Harlem, I think of the famous black people like Cab Calloway, Lena Horn, Ella Fitzgerald, Eartha Kit, Nancy Wilson and so many other amazingly talented people. These people have made it to the history books. They were famous then and still are. They were and still are famous entertainers and to me, their talents will never be duplicated.

There were a lot of opportunities for black people in Harlem in the 1940's."Colored people" is what we were called back then. This sounds almost funny now. I know this because my birth certificate says "colored" for my race. I never liked that. It is hard to explain why I don't like that term, but I don't. In those days, the term "colored" was a derogatory term for black people. It was not meant to dignify the black man as the person or human being, even though we worked hard and cared for our children. In fact, this term had the opposite effect. It was meant to be demeaning in how it was used and how it was presented. To me, I felt like less of a person if I was called "colored." If I had my way, everyone would only be called by the name that their parents gave them. That says who you are, not the color of your skin.

Ma talked about the early days in Harlem with much admiration. I think she really enjoyed herself. There was plenty of good shopping deals and amazing entertainment, too. Daddy and Ma would frequent the Apollo Theater. They would see some of the great black entertainers of the time, like Redd Foxx.

Wednesdays was amateur night, giving local black talent a place to get a break into show business. Ma said all the famous black people got started at the Apollo Theater. Back then, black people were not allowed to play in the fancy places like the Carnegie Hall and many of the clubs in downtown Manhattan. This went on for quite some time, said Ma. The Apollo Theater was on 125th Street in Harlem. Ma said every now and then she would go to a nightclub with Daddy, for a night out on the town. They would talk, and Daddy drank and danced with Ma. They had good times then.

Ma's younger brother moved to Harlem soon after my parents were married. He got married giving Ma a brand-new sister-in-law to pal around with. Ma was considered tall at 5 feet 7 inches and her sister-in-law was about 5 feet. They loved to shop together and were quite a good team. One was short and one was tall. They could see trouble coming from both angles. Because of the differences in height they avoided having their purses snatched. Ma saw the snatcher coming and my Aunt fought him off. What a team.

To me Harlem sounded exciting!I just love to think about the way everyone dressed. There is just one word to describe it - elegant. Because of the way New Yorkers dress, I am obsessed to this day with matching colors. I can't even take out the garbage without matching my attire. My mother always matched her clothing and I mean everything had to match - the shoes, the hat, the gloves, everything. My clothing was then and is still today color coordinated at all times when I'm outside the house. My California friends tell me that this need to color coordinate is a sickness that I have. They just never lived in New York City. Too bad for them.

There were several things that encouraged Daddy and Ma to move from Harlem. One major event was when the building next door caught fire and the flames spread to Daddy and Ma's building. Daddy was working at the time, but my oldest brother got Ma and her other children out of the building. It seems their neighbors, an older lady and her granddaughter, had started the fire by accident. A mattress caught fire and the granddaughter thought she had put it out, but it flared up and the fire department had to come and make sure the fire was totally out.

Ma's building had water damage and lots of smoke. At that time, Ma had six children in what she called her "railroad apartment." She called it this because all the rooms were in a straight line, just like railroad cars. I'm not sure I want to be trying to get away from a fire in an apartment like that.

Ma must have had similar thoughts. It wasn't all that long until they added more children, bringing the total to six and pretty much making the two-bedroom flat out of the question. Ma put her foot down that she just needed more room.

Shortly after baby number six was born they found a house to Ma's liking in Queens, New York. Ma actually picked the house out herself. It was on a nice block with a house on our left and right side and three houses across the street. It was very private, for New York City. By now Ma didn't have much time for neighborhood gossip or socializing. There were ten of us now and there was not much privacy for her in the home, so it was important that she really like her house.

Daddy always reminded us that when he bought this house, he felt like he had just signed his life away. He walked away with 50 cents in his pocket, six kids and a wife. I'm number seven and was the first born in Queens. You remember, it was on the coldest day of the year.

CHAPTER 3

I wasn't' supposed to be here. Ma wanted baby number five to be her last child. As you will soon discover, that just isn't how it went. Not only am I here, as baby number seven, but I have three younger siblings. Like I said, there were ten of us, and we were what you might call an active bunch.

As a matter of fact, I remember from the days before I went to school that Ma had help from a lady named Miss Richards. It must have been too much work for Ma, staying home and raising so many children. Daddy worked numerous jobs, so he wasn't home much in the early days.

The one thing I remember most about Miss Richards was the wonderful chocolate cakes she would make. These cakes were delicious and much to be desired. They were almost good enough to keep us kids from getting in trouble. Notice I said "almost."

Our days with Miss Richards were pretty consistent. She would get me and my sister Gail ready for the day and put us outside in the backyard to play before naptime. This went on in winter, spring, summer, and fall. Fortunately, we stayed inside on freezing days in the winter. I thought it was boring, but Gail and I would make up games and loved to play.

Things around our house were pretty stable. Ma stayed home and Daddy went to work. I only saw Daddy when he was going to bed or going to one of his jobs. Then one day the time came for me to go to school. I was nervous about school. What I picked up from my older sisters was that it could be stressful at times. I just wasn't ready for school. I would have just as soon stayed home. Besides how was I going to learn my ABCs? I just knew this was going to be a difficult task. But the good news was that Ma was still at home to greet me when I got back. What a relief.

CHAPTER 4

Kindergarten was easy. Much to my surprise I actually liked kindergarten. But then life got weird between kindergarten and first grade or second grade. Ma had another baby and she went to work soon after he was born. I guess by then Ma was tired of staying at home and just had to get out of the house. But to me this was a life altering experience.

Ma went to work on the graveyard shift at a hospital. This really changed my routine because I couldn't go to school until Ma got home from work each morning. I would sit with my little brother until Ma got home. As you might expect, I was always late for school - maybe ten minutes late. Ma going to work helped Daddy out. Even though Daddy didn't like it at first, Ma still went to work. Eventually Daddy was able to get down to one job, the one he retired from, working at the railroad.

Around my family, I was considered the quiet one. I didn't say much at home. Everyone else did the talking. I did the listening and watching. There was a lot to see and hear.

At an early age I realized education was a big deal to my father. I may not have been sure why we had to get good grades, but we did. If you had something less than a B on your Report Card, you were in trouble. No matter what the reason, you had to come home with As and Bs.

I usually got good grades and I never got in trouble with Daddy, at least not because of my grades. I was pretty intelligent and so were all my siblings. I felt that we were as smart as Martin Luther King's kids. I say that because Martin Luther King was a leader for blacks in the 60's and I would expect nothing but smart kids to come from him.

From an early age I wanted to be a journalist, but not the kind that was on all the TV news programs. I wasn't interested in being a news reporter. In fact, I did not like the news. I just knew I wanted to write. I told one of my older sisters I wanted to become a journalist but got no encouragement there. Maybe that was because she didn't know what she wanted to do with her life.

I started my first book in the fourth grade. Or was it the fifth grade. Anyway, I stopped writing it because my only subjects were kids in my class and there was a lot of drama at school. I didn't like writing about that sort of drama then, so I quit the book.

From an early age I tried to keep a journal, but I was not good at keeping up with it. I would start and do it well for a while, then I would stop. I think it was because there was no one offering encouragement about my writing. No one really knew about my love of writing and I put it on the back burner for a long time.

In my family I must say there was very little encouragement going around. It was more of an "every man for himself" environment. Maybe there were just too many of us to really care about what the other person was doing. As long as it didn't affect the other person personally, no one acted like they cared. But in reality everyone cared.

I remember writing a play for school one year. I think it was the fourth grade. The teacher helped a lot and the class actually preformed the play. No one made a big deal about it. There was another girl that helped with the play. It had something to do with the 1960s song *Age of Aquarius*.

As I mentioned, Daddy never explained to me why I should get good grades. I just knew I better not come home with bad grades. I did well in grade school, not really knowing why I was there. I didn't understand education, and its value, until I was an adult. How sad!

Being in the New York City public schools had its dangers. In the first grade, a girl tried to bully me. It was during the first week of class and I really didn't understand why this was happening since I didn't even know the girl. I was just playing with my new friends and here, out of the blue, comes the bully. She went straight for my pigtails and she wanted to pull my hair. My first thought was, "Oh boy, get me out of here." I couldn't understand that at all. Fortunately, one of my older sisters came to my rescue, saving my poor pigtails from who knows what. That was my first lesson that school was cruel.

Through it all, I still managed to get good grades, but something strange happened when I learned about death. It was weird. We got all dressed up one day. I thought we were going out to eat. In those days people got dressed up when they went out to dinner. Anyway, we were heading to an open casket wake. Daddy's uncle had died and as a family we went to view the body. There was no warning, what a shock. This dead person, whom I barely knew, was lying in a casket with a smile on his face. I figured that whether he was happy or not, there was no way I was trading places with him, even if he was having a good time in heaven.

No one in my family or among my friends knew it, but this experience got my mind going in a whole different direction. Pretty soon I was wondering if I would die in my sleep. I had heard that you could do that. I was scared to go to sleep at night for a long time. But every morning there I was, alive and well. Eventually my worries went away, and I got back to being another young girl in New York.

Life really changed for me in the fifth grade when I suddenly become rebellious. This was not a case of raging hormones; this is me realizing that one day I was going to die. I figured, I'm going to die anyway, don't really know when, so why can't I live my life doing what I want to do?My fifth-grade reasoning was telling me that I am here for a little while on earth, born to die, so why not live my own life and do what I want. This sure sounded logical to me.

Now I had a new reason to wonder why it was so important to do well in school. If I was just going to die anyway, why bother. It didn't make sense to me. Oh boy, what confusion I had in my head. And the sad part about it is that, these concerns stayed in my head. I figured that no one would believe that I had such concerns in the first place, so I kept them to myself. That was not hard to do in our family, where it was mostly every man for himself.

Maybe it was part of being rebellious, but fifth grade was also the time when I was introduced to partying. No, not those kiddy parties, I really partied. My classmates would have these adult-like parties, and everyone in the class was invited. When I say adult-like I mean the party was in someone's basement or garage. We would be in the dark and dance with the opposite sex. We would fast dance and slow dance. These parties would start in the afternoons around three and wouldn't end until around nine or ten at night.

I'll never forget my first slow dance with a boy. I was so nervous. As a matter of fact, I was always nervous when I went to one of these parties. I was so nervous I literately shook. So why did I go? Well two reasons; first, my parents let me go, and if you wanted to party and your parents said "yes," you went. Second, everyone else was going. Peer pressure.

We did a slow dance that was called the Grind. Now the Grind was a very nasty dance. In fact, if you remember the movie 'Dirty Dancing,' the Grind made that movie look tame. The boys would hold you so tight you couldn't breathe and put their hands on your back. The dance consisted in grinding your body parts together, VERY SLOWLY. This made me so nervous that I would actually shake in my shoes. I don't think any of the boys were nervous, but they may have been.

I've wondered why my parents let me go; after all, I was only ten. Not only that, I was not allowed to actually date a boy until I was seventeen. We'll talk about that later. Why was I allowed to go? The only conclusion I come to is that my parents did not actually know what was going on at those parties.

So back to our parties. We were in the dark until we heard an adult coming down the stairs, then someone put on the lights. As soon as the adults were gone, the lights went out. Some of the parties were in a living room or a garage. It was really an adult setting and I was not ready for that kind of party at the age of ten.

These parties pushed me to grow up faster than I wanted to. I'm not sure I realized this, since I just would have died if I couldn't go. That was the sort of peer pressure I was up against. You just weren't popular if you didn't go to these parties. So, I went, nervous feelings and all.

Fifth grade had more than its share of low points too. As if it weren't enough that I became focused on death, our fifth-grade teacher was, how should I put this, he was not very good. As a matter of fact, very few students bothered to listen to him. We pretty much did little or no class work. There was, however, a great deal of playing, joking, and general misbehaving.

Never being one to miss an opportunity, I became one of the class clowns. I didn't care. I would get lots of laughs. No one sat in the chairs; we all sat on the desks. When I should have been gaining an education, I choose an unfortunate role. Being one of the class clowns made me popular, and I liked it. I traded good behavior for popularity. We heard that the teacher had a nervous breakdown and had to leave. The school must have heard about our bad behavior because our next teacher could only be described as mean.

This new teacher was not playing around. I'm not even sure "mean" covered the situation. All of a sudden there was no talking, no goofing around, and we were actually expected to pay attention. If you were caught talking, you had to stay after school. I admit that I was always staying after school. She would catch me talking almost every day. Even so, I learned a lot more from this teacher. You could hear a pin drop in her classroom.

Ma never quite caught on to what was happening at school. She thought I was staying after class to help my new teacher. That's probably because that was the excuse I gave her for coming home late. Anyway, with all the things she had to do, one less child in the house was no big deal. Remember, I was the quiet one at home, so I was usually not missed.

Not only did I have a mean teacher that year, but I finally came to the attention of one of the local bullies and got beat up really bad. The bully's name was Shirley and she had already been kicked out of school. But Shirley would come around and beat on any girl in my class that she could catch off guard. It seemed like if she had enough time, she would beat or terrorize every girl in my class.

Then one day it was my turn. Shirley was actually looking for another girl named Tracy. Well, Tracy had not arrived at school yet. Shirley looks around, sees me, and says, "You didn't come to me that day I called you!" When Shirley called you, you did <u>not</u> go to her and you would hope she doesn't see you later. Well, since Tracy was not there, I knew I was in for a beating. I should have ran. Shirley beat me so badly, she actually knocked me out. When the yard monitor lady broke up the fight, I immediately started crying. I don't really remember much about the fight, but I remember the pain afterward. I remember this bully was trespassing. She didn't even go to our school.

Finally, graduation arrived. For graduation from elementary school we were told we could wear whatever we wanted. Well, we girls decided we would wear white or yellow dresses. I didn't get my dress till the day before graduation. I told Ma I wanted a yellow dress. Well Ma took one of my older sisters to go shop for my dress and they left me home.

How I wish they had let me go with them. They came back with a multi-colored dress. Spring colors! It was a pretty dress, so Ma wondered why I was having such a fit. Well you see, New York City was a fashion city at that time. You got looked up and down for fashion. I knew I was going to stand out like a sore thumb.

My older sister tried to make up for the situation by giving me a fabulous hairstyle. Well that was not good enough. Off to graduation I went, looking like a bouquet of flowers. There was nothing but white and yellow dresses, and then there was Joan in a multi-colored dress. I couldn't wait for it to be over. My younger sister Gail said I was the prettiest girl there. It didn't matter I hated being different.

Finally grade school is over!!!! What could be worse?

CHAPTER 5

My life in the neighborhood was separate from my school life. Not too many of my neighbor friends went to my school. My neighborhood buddies were like family. This gave me two sets of friends, neighbor buddies and schoolmates.

I was more loyal to my neighborhood friends. Like I said, we were like family. My neighborhood friends all lived within five blocks of me - east and west, north and south. I loved visiting my neighborhood friends and hanging out with them. We played just about any sport you can think of. We laughed and joked around constantly. It was a lot of fun, making Queens "Fun City" for us. We laughed and laughed and laughed. I'm still friends with some of these people after more than forty years.

When I wasn't hanging out, I was in the house trying to watch TV. I watched a lot of TV. It was an escape for me. My house was full of noise all the time. Remember, at this age I was still the quiet one who didn't really join in the noise at home. I just listened or looked around or watched TV when Daddy wasn't at home. You see Daddy didn't like the TV on in the middle of the day.

Before I left elementary school, my grandmother moved in with us. This was Daddy's mother. Daddy fixed up the attic for her. By the time he was done it like a little one-bedroom apartment up there. Having my grandmother around, we called her Nanny, resulted in several memorable moments. One in particular always stands out in my mind.

One morning I was waiting to leave for school. Nanny had helped us get dressed and ready. It was a spring day, I was eleven years old, and one of my neighborhood buddies walked up towards my house. My sisters, brother and I were waiting to leave for school when my neighbor friend says right out loud that there was no such thing as Santa Claus. Well of course I argued with her and defended Santa Claus. Just as the conversation was getting going, I looked over at my grandmother certain that she would be supporting my thoughtful argument that Santa Clause was real. She just looked at me and shook her head. To my shock, she was in agreement with my friend. Oh no!

Well I was devastated to learn the truth about Santa. Santa was my last ray of hope. He had to be a genuine good person. I benefited from Santa Claus, as did my brothers and sisters. What was I to think now? My world crashed down around my eleven-year-old shoulders.

Now my family went all out for Christmas, except for Daddy. He did not seem to actually get into the

Christmas spirit. This may have been because when he was a little boy, he was very poor and only got an apple or an orange for Christmas. I felt sorry for him, but that shouldn't mean that there was no Santa.

I must be honest that there were hints that Santa wasn't real, but I did the only logical thing - I ignored them. For example, why was Santa's signature on the gifts the same signature as my older sisters?Did they write the same or did Santa tell her to sign his name on the gifts?I dismissed these questions quickly. Now to realize that there was no Santa Claus made me rebel even more at school. I tried to be good but couldn't. How could anyone accept such an awful thing as no Santa Claus?

Another strong memory is when I was baptized into my parents' religion. Oh, did I mention my parents were very religious?Well, I didn't want to get baptized but Ma said I had to. Keep in mind that behavior and attitude were not exactly my greatest strengths at this point in my life. It wasn't that I wanted to be bad; it just somehow followed me around.

Now back to the baptism. I figured that if I had to go through this, by some miracle I might actually do better at school with my behavior and attitude. My parents' religion was really scary to me and it was all about the Holy Ghost. This Holy Ghost made some people do some very strange things. People would fall down and cry. Some of the people would shout loud phrases in a language I had never heard. There was no way I wanted that Holy Ghost taking me over. I didn't want to lose control of myself and fall down. No way!In case you are wondering, my parents were Baptist.

Well to make a long story short, I did get baptized and it really didn't change me one way or another. I just focused on getting out of elementary school and on with my life. After all, Junior High School had to be better, right?

By the time I graduated out of elementary school I was really ready to enter the seventh grade. I truly believed that nothing could possibly be worse than elementary school. Even so, I was a little nervous because in Jr. High School you walk from class to class. How was I supposed to do that and keep up with where I was to go?

As elementary school graduation approached, my concerns grew. This was the beginning of school bussing and I didn't even know for sure where I would attend school in the seventh grade. These were turning into pretty scary times.

As if this weren't enough, something weird happened to me shortly after graduation. I became a new person, well sort of a new person. I had heard of this thing that was bound to happen, but I never discussed it with my mother. It was a girl thing. It didn't happen to boys. Why us, I would think. Boys have it so easy. Nothing happens to them. Well it happened to me the summer between elementary and junior high school. Why?Why?Why?

Now I had heard from friends and neighbors about this thing and I wanted to know more about it. I knew it had happened to my older sisters, but they didn't warn me about it. I guess it should have been up to my mother to tell me about it. Well without real warning, "it" just happened, making this the most horrible day of my life to date.

I didn't really know what to tell Ma. I mean I didn't know the proper thing to say to her. I told her

I was bleeding out of my butt. Well she was totally indignant, and I had no idea why.

Ma told me not to "fresh around." I was devastated because I didn't know what she meant. Now that I am older, she meant to stay away from boys. She had told one of my older sisters to instruct me about what to do about feminine hygiene. Well my sister really didn't want to do it, so she showed me something and was gone quick. I was devastated and felt so dirty. There was only one thing left to do and that was to cry. So, I cried and cried. Today I understand that Ma had eight girls. By the time she got to me number seven, I guess she was tired. At the time, I didn't understand. I cried and cried and felt dirty.

Junior High School, here I come.

CHAPTER 6

This feeling that something was wrong in my life just wouldn't go away. You see, I wanted to question some of the things my family was doing, our way of life, if you will. But ours was a very average American family; we did nothing out of the ordinary considering things in America at the time. You do not get any more "apple pie" than New York City.

It seemed like everyone just took care of their responsibilities the best they knew how. Right or wrong, it didn't matter. There were not as many family rules then as now. In other words, people did what they wanted in the privacy of their homes. They mostly didn't worry about what their neighbors thought. After all, it really wasn't any of their business, at least that's how it was at the time.

In an attempt to deal with my uncomfortable feelings, I chose the big dinner table on Sunday afternoon to voice my spiritual concerns - how appropriate, I thought. After all, we had just left church. One thing I didn't understand was why my family gossiped about just about everyone in the church. I didn't understand why everyone went to Church as if it was a fashion show. If you were not well dressed, you were looked down upon. Why didn't people go door to door, like Jesus did? And the big thing I didn't understand was how come they didn't teach the Bible and what was in it. Every week, just a few scriptures were read, and the Pastor would blow one scripture out of context for the whole time.

Oh, by the way, we spent hours in church, and I got nothing out of it.

No one had an answer for me, so I just went on rebelling. Some of my questions I kept to myself because I didn't want to get anyone upset. What was funny was that no one actually knew I was rebelling. If you remember my telling you, I was the quiet one. When I did say something, I would usually get a strange look or answer. I was certain that I was the last person they worried about, but in reality, I was the one they should have worried about the most.

By the time I was twelve, I had many secret questions inside of me. These were questions about life, and no one, at least no one in my household, was going to explain it to me. You were totally on your own about such things. Everything was just one big secret with no one to help if you wanted to discover the meaning of life.

There I was in this big family with no one to explain life to me. My family was certainly interested in a good education, the kind of education you got from school, but I didn't know why you needed a good education. That was part of that "meaning of life" no one bothered to explain. Not that I wasn't going to seek a good education, because when you are in Rome you do as the Romans. It seemed like everyone in the neighborhood wanted a good education. It took me years to finally understand why a good education is important, something I will discuss in a future chapter.

There I was with questions that no one could, or more accurately, would answer. I went on with my life, sad and rebellious on the inside. But fortunately, I took from my parents their sense of humor, and I used it to the best of my ability.

I was a hoot, like so many of my siblings. We were naturals at making people laugh. We made each other laugh so hard we would pee in our pants. It seemed like all of New York City was laughing. There were so many comedians. I hung out and laughed all the time. In my neighborhood there was always someone funnier than you were. I could make you laugh without even trying. Even so, my sense of humor was severely tested when I entered middle school, or Junior High School as we New Yorkers called it.

Oh my god! What a waste of my time, or at least that is what I thought. The start of Junior High was when my real bad attitude kicked in. I didn't understand these attitudes or why I had them, but for better or worse I just went along with the feelings.

Thanks to my new view on life I soon became one of the class clowns. My attitude was, "how dare you." How dare these teachers challenge me? If I didn't like them, I didn't listen to them, although I still had to get good grades because of Daddy. So, I mostly did the work and even enjoyed some of it. But you can believe that when I didn't enjoy the work, the teachers knew about it. My "how dare you" attitude was in full display. With each day I approached some of my teachers thinking, "I know you get paid to do this work, but I can't wait to be grown up when no one is going to tell me what to do."

Foul language had become a big part of my regular speech. Some of this increased rebellion was because my class was the first class to be bused out of our neighborhood into an all-white neighborhood. Up till then I had seen white people, on TV mostly, but had very little experience with them. As a part of our school lessons, we were made aware of the struggles of black people in America since the time of slavery. These lessons made a huge impression on our fresh young minds so you can probably understand why we were a little ticked off.

Picture this, two busloads of black kids being bussed into an area with about a thousand white kids. A little exaggeration. To this day I remember saying out loud as we lined up for our brand-new school, "They all look alike." Oh, how awful that felt in the moment, but that was my America. We stood out like a fist full of sore thumbs. It shouldn't be hard to understand why some of us became very prejudiced.

Most of the children in my new school were Jewish, and they didn't like the German children. But there were also Irish, Italians, and who knows what else. But to me, they were all just white kids. And that's how my Junior High School got started. Days full of attitude and prejudice. Yes, we knew that we were the minority. We couldn't help it. That was just the way America was in the 1960s and early

1970s. And through it all, they kept telling me that a good education is all you need. I figured I had a better reason to be rebellious.

Everyone has something in their school career that they are not proud of. Mine was the time I and a few others incited a riot at school. That's right, little me - 80 pounds soaking wet. This was a well-planned disturbance. One of my friends actually created a bunch of posters and we put them up in the stairwells of the school. The posters said that the Black Panthers, a notorious black militant group, were coming up to our school at three o'clock. Needless to say, the school took us very seriously and had police at the school by three. To this day I think about this and believe that because we black kids were bussed in, we were the target of racism. The reaction of the school and the police just reinforced this belief.

There is always that one teacher you really didn't like. Well, I made the mistake of calling my least favorite teacher the "B" word. She wrote my father a letter in red ink, detailing my disrespect. In my defense, I told Daddy I said she was a "witch" and she just heard me wrong. Not surprisingly, that didn't work, and Daddy was really mad. We called spankings beatings back in the day and Daddy delivered a beating that lasted me for the rest of the year.

In Junior High, revenge can be sweet. On the last day of school, I threw a water balloon at this least favorite teacher. I was in the hallway when we were changing class and threw the balloon right at her. It hit her and I did not wait to see the damages. I took off running because there was no way I wanted a repeat beating from my Daddy. Fortunately, none of the kids in the hallway told on me.

Another example of my rebellious period was when I helped start a food fight in the cafeteria. It is funny, but I don't really remember what started the food fight, just that the food was flying from one end of the cafeteria to the other. What an amazing lunchtime that was.

I remember lying to my mother a lot during Junior High School. I dealt with my mother all the time because Daddy was not approachable. In fact,

Daddy did not want us to approach him when he was home. He wanted it quiet and that is how he got it. My home was so quiet when he was home that you could actually hear a pin drop. That was pretty amazing, given that there were ten kids in the house. Momma trusted me because I was quiet in the house. That was either a big mistake or she just didn't want to deal with me either. I was always late from school, mostly because I had finally discovered something interesting in Junior High School. You guessed it – BOYS.

It seemed like everyone else had a boyfriend, so why not me. I stayed with my first boyfriend throughout Junior High School. I finally ended it at the end of the eleventh grade. What an experience.

At first it was fun. This boy actually treated me with respect. He also was my protector. I mean no one bothered me without answering to him. We held hands a lot when we walked. He was nice to me and he was pretty popular, too. He was on the basketball team and it was nice to have a special friend who treated you like you were a lady. Unfortunately, I had to sneak around so my parents didn't find out. My parents did not allow me to date anyone. This was so stressful, all the sneaking around. My parents knew nothing about him.

By the end of the last year of Junior High School he was already begging for sex. I really wanted to do the "right" thing. What was a young girl with no family to talk to supposed to do? I had no desire to have sex.

One of my Junior High School teachers was a male sex education teacher who made it sound almost easy. He taught us that abortion is not killing a baby. According to him, abortion was just removing a little dot. He also taught us about birth control. Let me clarify that. He taught us that the rhythm method would keep us from having babies. It is probably no big surprise that I got pregnant. I believed black girls in my class got pregnant and had abortions before they were in High School. I believed some practiced rhythm method. Some of them got caught after graduation like I did. This is my belief, not on actual facts.

In 1973 abortions were legalized in New York City. Since I was one of those "rhythm methods" girls, I made the trip to a doctor for abortion number one. My older sister helped me get it. Daddy and Ma would have beaten it out of me if they had learned I was pregnant. It was so unfair. I'm almost sure some of us got pregnant because of that sex education teacher. Or should I just speak for myself. I wish I could sue that school today. What he taught was wrong on so many levels.

As long as we are discussing my delinquent youth, let's not leave out my playing hooky from class. I played hooky maybe three times. Well I got busted one time and the punishment was very severe. Daddy was not told about it, but Momma punished me and my sister Gail, who was with me on the hooky expedition, by limiting our time to hang out with friends that summer. We went out at noon and had to be back in the house by three o'clock. That was the worst summer I can remember.

Hanging out with my neighborhood buddies was my "to die for" life. We had so much fun; mostly played sports, all sports. My favorite was handball. I was good at handball. The Queens girls were known for handball throughout the city of New York. There was always someone to hang out with in New York.

I don't care what time of day or night it was you could find one of your friends to hang out with. We hung out at school playgrounds, parks, in front of each other's houses, in people houses, on street corners at night, in people's basements. You name it, we hung out there. We would just make each other laugh mostly.

We were busy evolving the latest and the greatest sayings of the day. Let me explain. New Yorkers had a sayings for just about every subject. There was always some saying or some song that people would make up. These sayings would ring a certain amount of truth in everyday life experiences. We were good about making up sayings. For instance, I truly believe that my sister invented the saying, "Tough Titties."

Anyway, graduation time was fast approaching. Yes, I graduated from Junior High and they were glad to see us go. No more busing that I know of at that school. We were the first class of bussed kids to graduate from I. S 25. I guess that was a big deal but to tell the truth, I was glad it was over. Right after Jr, High was over I had the rhythm method sex. He begged for 1 year. The crying made me give in to him. We all got split up to different High Schools around the Queens area. I was sent to the school in my neighborhood, which just happened to be the worst High School in Queens - just my luck. Back in the 1970s, Andrew Jackson High School was well known for student bad behavior.

I was back in my neighborhood for High School. That was the good news. The bad news was that Andrew Jackson High was the worst high school in the district. I needed that like I needed a hole in my head.

At least I still had my boyfriend from Junior High. We were still together but growing apart. He had not been what you might consider a good influence on me. He and his sister had introduced me to marijuana and by the time we entered high school he was also an alcoholic. I didn't much like drinking, but pot; now that was a different matter.

The first time I tried pot nothing happened. The second time was a totally different matter. I was totally high and couldn't stop laughing if I wanted to, which I really didn't. I thought this is the best thing that ever happened to me. Thanks to the pot, I could forget the lies, the abortion, school, church, and last but not least, what was going on in my house. Not that anything weird was going on in my house. Remember that we were the average American dysfunctional family.

In pot I had found a cure for what made me sad, but in reality, I became a worse person in the process. It seemed like I skipped the whole eleventh grade. The only classes I went to were the ones that I was pretty sure I was going to pass. If I knew I was going to fail a class, I wouldn't go. Instead I hung out at the handball court in the spring and my boyfriend's house in the winter. His parents were at work - perfect, I thought.

By now I was really hooked on marijuana. It was amazing how quick it happened. From this point I smoked pot every day for fourteen years. I was sure that I couldn't cope without a joint. How I passed to the twelfth grade I'll never know. My two best friends didn't pass. Given my grades, I stopped showing my report card to my parents, an accomplishment that is another great mystery to this very day.

Figuring out the best way to avoid school all together was my next goal. Turned out it wasn't all that hard, given the tracking system used by the school. If you didn't go to the homeroom class, you were marked absent for the day. Simple enough - I went to the homeroom class every day. The teachers in my classes would mark you absent for each class that you didn't attend and you were considered cutting that class because you had been present for your homeroom class. Now here is the kicker. They only sent a note home when you missed homeroom class. Once I figured this out, I knew I could cut class with little or no consequences.

There was one time I asked my sister to catch an absentee note for me. I had missed homeroom class and was marked absent for the day. If Daddy or Ma got it from the mailbox I would have been in big trouble, since they thought I had gone to school on that day.

Well my older sister agreed to shortstop the absentee note, but she made a big deal about it, as only a big sister can. She carried on and on and I was almost sorry I asked her. Anyway, she tampered with the mail and my parents never got the note. Then my sister made it clear that she would never do that for me again. That was OK by me. The note was destroyed, and I had gotten away with it, at least that what I thought.

There wasn't a lot of motivation to succeed coming from my teachers either. Some of my teachers would actually say that if you showed up for class, they would pass you. That's all I needed to hear to know enough to go to their class, not that they required I pay attention or actually learn. School to me was just a place to go for the day. I had no motivation to excel.

As you may remember, no one had actually explained to me why I needed to be there. I didn't know why I was there or what good I would get out of it in the long run. For the most part, the teachers were just collecting a check. I did, however, have one teacher from Andrew Jackson High that stands out in my mind even now.

This was my biology teacher and she did something really neat. One Saturday, she accompanied some of the students to the Natural Museum of History in New York City. We even went back to her apartment in Manhattan for pizza after the tour of the museum. That was so neat. I invited my boyfriend and I wish

I hadn't because by then we were growing apart. I was maturing and to me he was standing still. This teacher did try to motivate her students, unlike those who were just collecting a paycheck.

Each day started in the school bathroom with a cigarette and a joint. Remember, I was pretty sure I could not get through the day any other way. The drug dealers just camped out in the bathroom and made a lot of money. Plenty of people were buying joints. We thought we ruled the school. Security was a joke and the teachers were scared of us, well some of them.

Marijuana was truly my downfall. It made me lazy and very selfish. I never wanted anything else but to be high. The marijuana was everywhere. The users stood out like sore thumbs. We may have thought we were cool cats, but in reality, we were dumb cats. School didn't mean anything to me. I was a rebel. You could always tell who used marijuana because our eyes were very blood shot. To fix that, we used Visine eye drops, especially before we went home. You see we had the kind of weed that kept you high all day.

CHAPTER 7

Something terrible happened to me in the eleventh grade. I had a nervous breakdown. I had been carrying a heavy burden for three years inside me - my abortion.

The abortion was supposed to be a big secret, but it leaked out little by little. Before I knew it, some seemed to know my deepest, darkest secret. I was so ashamed and thought about it every day until one day it felt as if I just burst, landing me in the hospital. I guess if you think about something everyday all the time for three years and never tell anyone about your thoughts - not even the person that caused you to get pregnant - it's going to end badly.

Life in the 1970's was very different than now. If people found out you had been pregnant, you were quickly labeled a "hoe." That was neighborhood talk for the sort of girl none of us wanted to be. God forbid if they found out you had an abortion. People would talk about you like you were a dog. This treatment wasn't just for those who had abortions. If you were having sex with your boyfriend and people found out, they also labeled you a "hoe."

Sex was private and people were supposed to be kept to themselves. We did not discuss our relationships with others. People knew you had boyfriends, but you never discussed the intimate details with other people. It was sort of like there was a line drawn and everyone respected the other person's privacy. But if your business got out, you were quickly labeled, and not in a good way.

When I suspected word of my abortion got out, some people gossiped about me. Even 2 my sisters called me a "hoe" when they found out. That was so hurtful especially when I thought that they were having sex with their boyfriends too. Things got so bad that I stopped talking to one sister for three years and another for one year. It was terrible being treated this way; all because I was no longer a virgin. You see people in New York City wanted you to believe that they were as pure as the driven snow. That was so phony.

To make matters even worse, I found out that it was one of my siblings who actually leaked the big secret. Can you imagine that? To make matters worse, everybody just kept talking about it behind my back. There was only one person who told me he had heard about it. No one else had the guts to approach me about it. Being talked about like that, especially as a teenage girl, was awful. I hated the feeling of being exposed in my own neighborhood. Although not approached about it.

What made matters worse was that I never wanted to do it in the first place. Sex with my boyfriend was disgusting. It was disgusting because everything about it was strictly for his pleasure. I got no satisfaction out of it. When he wanted it, he got it, and whenever I was near him, he wanted it. I thought that as his girlfriend it was my duty to give it to him. I really can't remember ever wanting it for myself. I was so dumb and went along with him. That's why I think it was disgusting. I did something I didn't want to do. He knew I was not getting anything out of it, but he didn't care.

The reasons I had sex with him in the first place was because he begged me. Looking back, I see how sad that was, to beg for sex for almost a year. His hormones were raging. When I finally gave in and had sex with him. The crying made me do it. This was my breaking point. From that time on I just couldn't say no to him.

We had set a date and time and we did the deed. I had paid enough attention in Health class to know about birth control. We agreed on the rhythm method, but his raging hormones assured that was never going to work. Low and behold, I got pregnant. After all that drama and emotion, I ended up having to get an abortion for something I didn't even want to do in the first place.

At two months pregnant I told one of my older sisters about my problem. We took a walk down the street and I delivered the news - she cried. I told her not to tell Ma and Daddy and that I wanted an abortion. Remember, I was taught in school it wasn't really a baby at that early stage of pregnancy. I just knew if Ma and Daddy knew about it, they would have beat the baby out of me. So, my sister agreed not to tell anyone and to help me get an abortion.

It was the summer of 1973. Abortion had just become legal in New York City. In one sense, this relieved me of a lot of pressure. On our chosen day, my sister pretended she was taking me shopping and I went and got the abortion. It was a Saturday and we went to Manhattan. I was the youngest one in the clinic to get the abortion that day. I was fifteen but I looked twelve years old, at least that is what the nurses said.

My fetus was just two months along, so I qualified for what they called a local procedure. That meant that I was awake through the whole thing. It took them just three minutes to suck that baby out of me. Being young and focused on myself alone, I felt relieved. I rested at the clinic for a while and then went home. I had cramps for a short time, but they went away, which is more than I can say for the guilt.

My sister took me out to eat after the abortion and I swore I was done with sex forever.

My sister had paid for the abortion, which was $250. It was agreed that I would pay her back. Given his participation in getting me pregnant, I passed this information on to my boyfriend, suggesting that he pay for half the cost. No shock here, but he never did pay. I eventually paid my sister back, but it was not until I was 19 years old. That was a debt I just couldn't refuse paying.

CHAPTER 8

My "big event" began one Sunday afternoon after church when everyone was in a good mood. I was in my usual place in front of the TV. This time I was playing checkers with one of my nieces, watching the TV from the corner of my eye. Out of the blue, I fell backwards, and my eyes rolled to the back of my head. I even swallowed my tongue. The family rushed me to the hospital. To this day I believe that the fear of my parents learning about the abortion was what pushed me over the edge. After all, I was definitely guilty and ashamed of myself.

They rushed me to Long Island Jewish Hospital. Daddy thought I was on hard drugs, but I wasn't. I may have been a dumb kid, but I wasn't stupid. Fortunately for me, the marijuana didn't show up in the blood stream on the test that they gave me to see what caused the seizure. Guess I had to get lucky sometimes.

They diagnosed me as having had a nervous breakdown. Not exactly the way I wanted to spend my seventeenth year. The doctors wanted to know the reasons for my condition. Not so with my family. They knew what some of the reasons could have been. After all, I wasn't exactly an innocent child at home. I was pretty pushy, always insisting on having things my way with my siblings. Most of my relatives will tell you that I was a bit of a smart mouth.

But some of the times I was good and fun around my siblings. Even given my attitude issues, I still think people should be more honest and open to one another, or at least approachable, with family. Most of my siblings kept their private life private and just pretended they weren't doing anything but work and school. We had fun together and laughed a lot, but like I said, personal things stayed personal, not to be talked about.

But that was bad for me because I wanted to be open and honest with my siblings about important things in my life. I have been told by family members that at this age I would say just about anything that came to my mind. But like I said, things were just not talked about. Many in my family pretended nothing was going on but work and school. It was taboo to speak openly and honestly on almost any intimate subject. The code in my house was "Hush Hush!" That was the dysfunctional part.

After my breakdown I ended up in the hospital for three months. One of the first things that Ma told me was, "Don't tell them anything about your father." Daddy was a bit of a tyrant, for lack of better words. I listened to Ma and never told them anything about Daddy. Needless to say, I never really got better.

Ma's advice probably didn't matter anyway, even though I followed it. Daddy's ways weren't really the reason for my breakdown. It took me quite a few years, but I eventually figured out that it was the abortion that pushed me over the edge.

As if life weren't crazy enough, while I was in the hospital, my father finally agreed to let me have a boyfriend. Remember, I'm seventeen at the time. This was so unfair. Some of my siblings had boyfriends when they were younger than me.

So here comes my boyfriend to visit me in the hospital. This is the same boyfriend who had gotten me pregnant earlier and sent me off to the abortionist. Unbelievably, he arrived at the same time Daddy was visiting me. Talk about a little awkward.

Earlier I had told him on the phone that I couldn't have any glass in my room because I was in the psych ward where I was supposed to stay a couple weeks. What does this fool do? He brings me flowers in a glass container. I freaked out over the glass vase. He had tried to cover it up with aluminum foil, but that didn't help. Not only does he break the rules with a glass vase, he arrives when Daddy is sitting right there. I just about had a fit. Unfortunately, the hospital attendants saw my reaction. So much for a short two week stay - I ended up in that hospital for three months. I even had to attend school while I was in that place. In a way it was funny that they actually had a school for the nervous breakdown children. That was crazy New York City.

As you might imagine, freaking out like that in front of my father and my boyfriend at the same time was devastating. I have to say that falling apart in front of Daddy was actually the worst. Yes, he was a bit of a tyrant, and yes, he was unapproachable to everyone. What is amazing, however, is that with all these daughters, none of us was "Daddy's little girl." He was hard on each of us.

When Daddy was home you could hear a pin drop no matter how many kids were in the house. Frankly, we were all scared of him. He had a bad temper and if he lit into you once a year the memory of the beating would last at least the entire year. I had heard he was abused as a child and that spilled over into how he treated his own children.

I had also heard that he was like that because there were so many of us. I truly believe that he tried to be nice to us and kid around, but no one took it seriously because we feared his dominant personality. Ma would regularly remind us that, "He is a good provider." The interesting thing is that because he was a hard worker, we all learned the value of working hard. It was nice how that worked out.

All this was happening while I was in eleventh grade, near the end of high school with all those "what will I do" questions looming out there. School was definitely not a favorite part of life, so I knew that I didn't want to continue my education immediately after high school. Funny thing was that I also knew that one day I would go back and attend college. At the time, I just wanted a break from teachers.

I justified these plans by thinking that after all, Daddy was a working man with a big house in Queens who raised ten kids without the help from the government. All he had was a high school education. I thought I would pattern myself after him. After all, I never really understood the big rush was to continue my education anyhow. After all, I was seventeen and pretty much knew it all, right?

CHAPTER 9

What I never expected was how my life was about to be shattered. At the young age of fifty-five, Daddy became disabled and could no longer work. He had developed diabetes and thrombophlebitis. This is where a blood clot blocks one of your veins. He had to retire from ERA Lackawanna Railroad in New Jersey where he had worked for a good long time.

Our family's life was turned round and round. Never mind that because of the diabetes everything in our pantry turned to diet, like sodas and sweets, we were actually moving out of the Big Apple - New York City. Can you imagine that?! I just couldn't. Daddy decided that he did not want to retire in New York City. This was a disaster for me. After all, I had passed from eleventh to the twelfth grade and was about to be a high school senior in the neighborhood I grew up in. No way did I want to leave now.

Like it or not, I had to understand that Daddy had worked very hard all his life and it had finally caught up to him physically. What I didn't understand was that he wanted to retire to his and Momma's hometown of Whatley, Alabama. OH MY GOD! This had been our regular vacation spot. It felt like just about everybody there was related to me one way or another. My party was definitely over!

It was the summer of 1975 and I was almost finished with school. One more year and I would graduate high school. Momma came to me with two options. I could stay in New York City and finish high school, or I could move down south and stay with them. Of the ten children, four of us were still in school. Reluctantly, I decided that I wanted to be with my Momma, so I choose to move to the great state of Alabama. Little did I know that Momma had other plans. She was going to stay in New York for most of that year to close and sell the house. If I had known that I would have made a much different decision.

In some ways, all of my Daddy's hard work actually paid off. He was able to have a brand-new house built on acres of land he had inherited from his family. He told me he would have had more land but that the white man took part of it from his grandfather.

Daddy paid the taxes on this land since he left Alabama in the 1940's. To be honest, I was glad they left Alabama before I was born. I would not have wanted to be raised down there. If you don't know the history of black people in the south in the first half of the 1900's you should look it up.

When we would visit my grandfather's house in the 1960's, my step grandmother would tell us not to look white people in the eyes. Being from New York City, I found that very strange but to this day it is hard for me to look anyone in the face. The south was not very nice to black people then. I'm glad it changed. I was not raised to fear a person because of skin color. Thank you, NYC!

I must admit that there was another reason, beyond being with Momma for my decision to move. I wanted to ensure that I was going to graduate from high school. You see, I had to pass all my classes in order to graduate from Andrew Jackson High School. Fail just one class and I was out of luck. This would have meant no playing hooky, no pot smoking, and no monkeying around. This did not appeal to me in the slightest. For I was so used to doing the opposite.

By this time, I had broken up with my boyfriend. Believe it or not, I thought he was immature. Given all you now know, it may make you laugh that I thought I had matured faster than him. We loaded up the truck and moved, but not to Beverly Hills that is, if you get my drift.

CHAPTER 10

Welcome to Alabama. Here I am seventeen and living in the middle of nowhere, just wall to wall woods. Ma stayed in Alabama long enough to get us settled, then she returned to New York. As the oldest child still living in the house, I became the new Ma. Boy did I have an attitude.

One of the only good things about moving to Alabama was that I had actually completed all my requirements to graduate high school, at least according to the State of Alabama. I didn't have to attend class at all. But I went anyway because I didn't want to stay home with Daddy. He was trying to make me into a farm girl. Can you imagine that? A girl from New York City becoming a farm girl.

Daddy worked us hard. He taught us how to plant rows of corn and God only knows what else. I think we planted peanuts and peas. We also had to kill this terrible vine called kudzu that grew in the south all over everyone's property. We had hogs to slop, that means feed them, chickens to feed, and even a cow, at least for a while. Daddy said I was good at farming and he wanted me to stay in Alabama. As far as I was concerned, that just was never going to happen.

The doctors in New York had told Daddy to rest, but he had headed down south to farm. I may have been pretty good working in the fields, but let's say this was not my favorite line of work.

Where do I start with that bad experience that is named Whatley, Alabama? What a culture shock. School was probably the biggest shock. We were picked up by a school bus full of crazy country kids. Please realize that crazy country kids are very different from crazy city kids. As if things weren't tough enough, my mother's first cousin drove the bus I was on and no one liked her. Anyway, the ride to school and back was hellish. I may have had a bad attitude but at least I knew I was going to leave after graduation. And that I did, three days after I graduated. But I'm getting ahead of myself.

Like many teenagers, all I cared about was myself. I would tune out the noisy bus and no one on the bus was a friend of mine. Not to say I wasn't at least somewhat sociable. Two of my cousins rode that bus and I was friendly with them, but mostly because we were kin.

These kids were jealous of me and my siblings. I guess because we were from NYC. This made them jealous and some of the kids on the bus wanted to fight me and my siblings. It was awful. But when they found out we weren't scared of them, they backed off. How I managed not to fight at least one of those kids was amazing.

The only thing those kids wanted to do was gossip – "Who shot Johnnie Raine?" "Did you see the ugly dress Nancy wore?" I just didn't care. The girls were actually more hateful and full of gossip than the boys, so I hung out with the fellas at school.

I'm just not a dramatic person. I just didn't care. I had one thing on my mind and that was leaving Whatley. Some of the kids had as much as we did, but the ones that had less really hated me and my siblings. One big point was that the poor kids had less clothing. Some didn't have coats to wear until

Christmas came around, then their parents bought them coats. I thought that was awful of their parents to wait for Christmas to buy them warm coats. It was cold long before Christmas!

My main reason for hanging out with the fellas was that they didn't gossip. And if I did talk to some of the girls, they would miss quote me and spread lies about me. Since the fellas made me laugh and the girls were kind of hateful, I stayed away from the girls.

I finally came to the conclusion that if I didn't find some sort of recreation, I would just die. After all I was a teenager. I could not drive and was not about to ask Daddy to teach me. I had seen his teaching technique when he taught my older sisters to drive. Being yelled at and scared half to death was not my idea of a good way to learn to drive. But I had to get out of the house somehow.

The answer came like a bolt from the sky - get a boyfriend with a car. So, I did. I actually stayed with him till graduation. Of course, I thought I loved him and wanted him to join me when I left for New York

City. As you might expect, he had other ideas about New York City and two weeks after I left Whatley, he had a new girlfriend.

This relationship was OK. He was two years older than me and we were civil with each other. We had a standing date on Friday nights and went out on Saturday nights to the Jute Joint. This is a place to dance. I danced, he didn't. Sometimes we would just hang out and he would drink beer and I would smoke. These events were usually at an abandoned house, which was fine since it gave me something to do. It was a routine. We also went to the drive-in movies. That was about it.

As I said earlier, I had enough credits to graduate High School in Alabama, which freed me up to turn my classes into one big nap. The only things I enjoyed in that school were breakfast and lunch. They really were good cooks in Alabama. I ate the food there and was glad to get it. Those were very tasty southern dishes.

Alabama has a reputation for good cooks. Everyone knew how to cook, and I never ate a bad meal at someone else's home. They love to feed you in Alabama. They were very hospitable people. We had a joke. When someone sees you coming up to their house they yell in a loud voice, "Come on in." One of my siblings and I would joke and say back, "in already."

People in Alabama loved to feed you. At least that's how it was back then. Food was definitely a high point for my stay in Alabama, eating at different relatives homes all the time. They were excellent cooks. They always welcomed me, even knowing that I didn't want to stay down there.

I may remember that the food in that Alabama school was really good, but that is not to say we didn't have good food at home. Momma was an excellent cook. Thanksgiving was coming up and everyone was anticipating the big meal we were about to have. Turns out it was one of the best Thanksgiving meals I ever ate. Granted it was served at lunch period.

CHAPTER 11

Graduation was coming fast, but first came the Prom. I'm sorry to say it, but I really hated the Prom. All that preparation…and for what? Mom made my dress and I must say I did look nice. It was a long white gown. My sister Gail was also supposed to go the same prom with her boyfriend, who was one of my classmates. She had the same dress I had but in blue. Gail is fourteen months younger than me, but we were very close – almost like twins. She never actually made it into the prom. Turns out they sat in my boyfriend's car all night. Gail's boyfriend was mad because he didn't get the suit he wanted to wear to the prom. What a dope.

One of my older sisters, who thought she understood me, came down from New York to attend my graduation.

My cousins from Birmingham came to visit while my older sister was there, and we had lots of fun together. There was a after-graduation party for my class. Just before I went into the party, I smoked a joint. I didn't know what to expect but I was way too high. As it turned out, the party was actually lots of fun, and it wasn't the weed either. But I knew I was not going to see my boyfriend again or the people that was at the party. For a while I felt a little sad. Then it hit me - Oh my God, what was wrong with me. I hated it down there.

I guess I should mention that the school created a special paper for the graduates and my name was mentioned several times. It wasn't for big things, most stuff like the color of my eyes and other things about me being nice. It really surprised me, since I thought I had kept a pretty low profile. I realized after I read the paper some of the kids liked me. I never knew it until then. What a shame.

Graduation day! Best I can say is that I was G-L-A-D happy. Even on graduation day, Whatley was a very memorable place. Being in the deep south, just a about every girl in my class had the name "Jean" as a part of her name, mostly as a middle name. As the principal called each student up to receive his or her diploma, he read off their full name, and there was a lot of "Jeans."

When he got to me, he read out "Jean Iola Pope." I thought I was going to just die. My face just dropped, and I whispered in his ear, "That's Joan Iola Pope. Not Jean." He corrected it right away, but I was still mad. At that very instant my Aunt snapped a picture of me frowning. It is funny now, but for a teenage girl, it was a tough way to end High School.

Just three days after graduation Daddy took me back to New York City. I think they were glad to see me go because I was so unhappy and a bit of a b---h! But that's ok, because NEW YORK CITY HERE I COME!

CHAPTER 12

I'll never forget the day Daddy and I arrived in New York City after I graduated from High school. You remember; I graduated in that small rural town in Alabama.

It was a pretty day at the end of May in Hollis, Queens, New York City. No, it was a beautiful day in Hollis, Queens, New York City. I think the weather made me feel like this was going to be a good move for me. After all, I believed that there was nothing better than Hollis.

Daddy's first stop was the preacher's house. Daddy was very close to this preacher because he was the co-founder of the preacher's church. I believe I was about three years old when they founded that church.

Given my past issues in New York City, I'm guessing that Daddy also wanted the pastor to pray for me.

Once that visit was over, we headed to the basement apartment of two of my siblings where I was to live. These two had rented a two-bedroom apartment from one of my mother's best friends. The apartment was nice enough, especially for a kid like me who was just out of high school. Daddy stayed with us for a while than he went to my older sister's house. By then, she had two children and lived in a nice house in Hempstead, New York, just east of my old stomping grounds in Queens. Having seen his friends and family for a brief while, Daddy decided it was time to return to Alabama.

My first act as a free woman in New York City was to visit the old neighborhood and look up all my old friends. You know, my running buddies. I loved the taste of freedom. I found the old gang just hanging out on the corner. You could tell from first glance what they were up to. Compared to them, I looked cleaned up and squared away. Did I stay that way? No, I did not. Like the young fool I was, I jumped right in and picked up where I left off.

As time went by, I did get homesick for Mother. Her words of wisdom kicked in. For instance, she would always say, "Ain't nobody stutting you." Which meant nobody was thinking about me. How true those words were to me at that time. I was truly on my own. People just cared for themselves and themselves only.

My plan was to get work first and then consider options for my further education. Back then, I didn't really know why I needed an education. I just figured that I needed money in my pockets. So off I went looking for a job, which I found right off. A local bank in Flushing, Queens hired me right away to be a teller. I worked Monday thru Friday, and on the weekends hung out with friends, partying and getting high. Everything was moving along just fine, except for one thing - I didn't have a boyfriend. At this time of my life I foolishly thought, "Exactly what are you without a boyfriend?" So, I went out and found one.

CHAPTER 13

For a while, I had a boyfriend and a sidekick, you know, a best friend, for when my boyfriend wasn't available. How I met my boyfriend was easy. I went to a college party at a University. It was a good party atmosphere and I met this guy the first night.

He and I hit it off right away. We would talk for hours on the phone. We went out a lot too. The most memorable night was when we went to see Ashford and Simpson in concert at a club in Manhattan called The Bottom Line. That's where he would take me on our dates - The real city. Manhattan was very exciting with plenty to see and do.

This boyfriend was a gentleman, or at least that is what I thought. He knew how to show a girl a good time. But when it came to college boys, I had just one rule. If you have a girlfriend at school, I'm not going up there. Well, he lied and said he didn't have a girlfriend at school. What a shock; a college boy lying to his girlfriend.

Seemed like the truth at first. I spent time with him in his dorm room where we would get high. Once in a while his buddies would come in the room to visit him. It was nice because I could tell that they approved of me. They wouldn't stay long, just a short visit.

Fortunately for us, his roommate was always gone for the weekend. I'm sure they had an understanding. On occasion I would go there on a weeknight. It really didn't matter because there was always a party at the student lounge.

Then one night it happened. His college girlfriend showed up. I was OK with his seeing someone else; so long as it was understood I was number one. Not so much with this other girlfriend. She was mad, screaming and wanting to see who I was. My boyfriend would kick her out of the dorm room, but she would come back screaming and calling me all sorts of nasty names.

She obviously thought I also went to the school. At one point I thought she was going to get passed my boyfriend, fighting with him at the door. Fortunately, he kicked her out of the dorm a third time and she quit coming back. Needless to say, I knew I couldn't trust him again. So that sweet relationship was going south. When we finally broke up, I was heartbroken. He was a pretty good boyfriend.

So, there I was in New York City without a boyfriend, again. I had to start looking for a man all over. Two of my best friends had boyfriends so it was awkward hanging out with them, my being a fifth wheel. But they let me tag along. We were close like that, they didn't mind, and besides, I had quite a few different best buddies I could hang out with at different times.

Things were not going well for me as far as joining the work force was concerned. I lost my job at the bank for not smiling enough, I guess. That's why I think they fired me, not the reason they gave – their reasons were bull.

They claimed that I lost $100 from my cash tray and that they couldn't find an error. I never lost any money in my transactions. It was a reason they used to get rid of me. They treated me so poorly that it is hard for me to smile even to this day. After that I went from job to job. I was really down about that. But I always would get a job. It looked like I was not going to have a real career in New York City.

CHAPTER 14

Here I am with no boyfriend and a bunch of different jobs. So, you might ask, how did I get pregnant at the age of 19? It came down to landing my own basement apartment and being desperate to find a boyfriend. I really just wanted sex. My hormones were raging.

I met what seemed like a nice guy on the city bus, so I gave him my sister's phone number. He started to call me, and we talked. He seemed nice enough. Remember, I'm a 19-year-old with raging hormones.

He would visit me at my apartment, but he would only stay for a minute or two. I was too dumb to put two and two together. More on this later.

One day I wanted sex and so did he, big surprise. I told him to please pull it out because neither of us had protection and I didn't want to get pregnant. Of course, he promised to pull out. Well he lied and I got pregnant. All of the sudden he gets all full of himself and says that he was a man and men do not pull out. What a crock!

Not long after that he took me to his mother's house to introduce me to her. She was not very happy about me and asked him what he was doing fooling around. This seemed odd but then so was his mother. Eventually I found out he was living with a woman. No wonder he never spent a lot of time with me. Duh!!!!

I confirmed that I was pregnant and when I told this guy he claimed it wasn't his. Now there was no one else in my life for the previous six months so I was highly insulted. As it turned out, I didn't even like him as I got to know him. To make things worse, I got kicked out of my cute basement apartment. Turns out the owner's son needed a place to stay after his wife kicked him out. Bye bye Joan.

My boyfriend may have claimed the baby wasn't his, but at least he helped me find a room to rent. It was a room in the house of his friend's girlfriend. When this no-good friend says he would convince his girlfriend to let me stay there for free, I jumped at the offer. After all, I didn't even have a job at that moment and very little cash.

What I didn't realize until it was too late was that in return for helping me get the room, my boyfriend's buddy wanted me to have sex with him behind his girlfriend's back. I didn't want to do it, but I really needed a place to stay. It was like rape for me. I hated it.

Clearly, I was headed for another abortion. When the day came for the procedure, I went into the hospital. To my total shock, there were the parents of my no-good boyfriend, the one who got me pregnant. The mother was checking his father in the hospital. I don't know if she recognized me or not; we didn't exchange greetings. New Yorkers do not exchange greetings unless they know you.

I had the abortion not even thinking it was a baby. When I got back to the boarding house, the two-timing rapist wasn't there.

It seemed like it was time to find a job and move on, which I did. I stayed on this job for several weeks. Finally, all my troubles caught up with me and I suffered another nervous breakdown. Guess I couldn't handle the pregnancy, abortion, boyfriend, job loss, and rapist all at once. I'm not sure many people could.

I was in the boarding house when it happened, and it was so bad that I ended up in the hospital again. My siblings were contacted about my condition after I was taken to the hospital. I was in such bad shape by then that they gave me Thorazine. This drug knocked me out for several days. I remember Uncle Charlie trying to wake me up, my fathers' half brother. But I couldn't move.

Then Momma came. Believe it or not, it was my birthday. I didn't realize it at the time until I saw the cake. Ma came all the way from Alabama to save me from myself. I was so glad to see her.

I stayed in the hospital for about a month. No one there told me what the problem was or how I could avoid these problems in the future, leaving it up to me to figure things out. Momma needed to get back home so she asked me if I wanted to go to California.

I had a sister there. I thought this was a good idea since I truly needed a change from the mess I had made of myself in New York.

I had failed, or so I thought. I spent two years in New York on my own and now it was time to slow my buns down. It was funny, but no one in my family asked me what had happened to me or why. Like I said, they had their own lives to worry about.

I think that Momma must have let the rest of the family have it a little over not taking care of me. It was the holidays and Momma didn't hear from me. So, she knew I was in trouble. When she asked my siblings where I was, they told her that they didn't know. After I moved out of my apartment, they lost track of me.

Looking back, that really was a tough thing to realize. This was a bad time for me, but I knew I could never have another abortion. That was the trigger for my despair. For two years I roamed on the streets of New York City without the benefit of my parents. I had totally failed at living on my own in that fast-paced environment.

I just couldn't make it on my own there. It seemed like everything I tried I failed at. I just didn't know how to survive and how to be happy at the same time. Boyfriends were definitely not the answer and my attempts at education had failed as well. This was just not my town after all. I tried to further my education I guess you really can't go home again. That part was sad, but I was happy to be getting out. There was a dark cloud following me around in New York City.

I needed the sunshine!!!!

CHAPTER 15

My escape from New York City was now under way, but a few days in Alabama sounded like a good idea. I had been away from Ma for a long time so that seemed like a good place to start.

I still owed rent to the lady that owned the boarding house. It was less than $300 so Daddy paid the lady off for me - he was always there when I needed him.

To tell the truth, I don't really remember how Ma and I got to Alabama. What I do remember was that I was off my rocker when I got there. I remember my little sister putting her arms around me and speaking consoling words to me and saying, "Let's go to bed Joan." I followed her advice and that was when I started feeling better.

Even though I had started to act more normal, Daddy wanted me to see a doctor there in Alabama. After all, Ma was about to take me to California.

This was another of those mysterious experiences that had become my life. We went to see the doctor and he prescribed some pills. It would have been nice if someone had told me what the matter was but handing out pills was what he was about. At least the doctor cleared me for travel because Ma and I were heading west.

Ma asked if I wanted to fly to California or take the bus. Well I didn't like flying so it was an easy decision to choose the bus. I knew the bus ride from Alabama to California was going to be a long one. Ma knew it too and explained my condition to the bus driver. Ma obviously didn't want us kicked off the bus if I said or did something strange. Ma knew I was capable of bringing some undue attention to myself and anyone around me.

Buses are usually places to meet "interesting" people. I met a nice couple that was moving to San Diego. They were probably in their mid-20s, a few years older than me. The reason they noticed me was because I almost got in a fight.

The problem, or at least what I thought was a problem, began when this guy put his feet on the arm of my mother's chair. In his mind he just wanted to stretch his legs. My mind was saying, "Not with your feet on the arm of MY mother's chair!"

First, I asked him nicely to remove his foot. Well, he wouldn't. So, I asked him again and little more firmly, and he refused again. I finally had to curse him out before he moved his feet. After this the couple that was going to San Diego befriended me. They thought that guy got what he deserved. To be honest, the guy probably thought I was some kind of nut, which technically I was. Even so, he moved those feet pretty darn fast.

My new friends were what you might call, "Children of that Age." They liked to smoke pot. They were also generous and gave me a marijuana joint to smoke in the bathroom. Wouldn't you know, I decided to smoke it when the bus was close to the Mexican border. The border guards came on board to check the bus, but thank heaven, I got out of the bathroom just in time.

One of the characters I remember from the bus was this lady who sat up in the front and had big curlers in her hair. When we stopped to get off the bus for various reasons, I always looked for Miss Curlers. That's how I knew we were on the right bus. I'd yell, "Hey Miss Curlers," which I must admit was not a nice thing to do. She spoke to the bus driver about my taunts, so I stopped. It would have been bad if I got us kicked off the bus. Seeing my actions through the eyes of an adult today, I do know how embarrassing this must have been for her.

All in all, the ride was fun, in my crazy sort of way. I was so manic at the time that I didn't really care how ridiculous I looked or sounded. I just wanted to keep busy. My friends helped here and kept me company. Good conversation too. If they were older, they would probably have been part of the Hippies. But they were too young, like me.

Finally, we arrived at San Diego and it was time for my friends to get off the bus. I would have gotten off with them if Ma wasn't there. San Diego was a beautiful spot. I really wanted to live there but it was not meant to be. We said our goodbyes and never met again.

CHAPTER 16

After an interesting, and sometimes eventful ride we finally arrived in Sacramento, California. It was a warm, peaceful, laid back 1978 evening. I looked around and decided that I was going to be good. Well, maybe.

My sister and her Man picked us up at the bus depot. My beautiful, five-year-old niece was with them. I knew right then that I needed this move so desperately. Now this man was not my ex-brother-in-law, but he seemed to be a nice man.

My sister lived in a very nice neighborhood called Lincoln Village. Not being one to waste a great deal of time, I figured this was a good time to start my new life. To begin with, I needed a job and a man, or that was what I thought. After all, what is one without the other? I found both right away and Ma was actually supportive of both. She made no mention of my condition. It was as if it had never happened. How strange!

Our early time in Sacramento was all about getting to know this great big place called California. First my sister and her Man took Ma to see Lake Tahoe for the day. I babysat my niece and when they got back, my niece and I sang a song to them that we had made up while they were gone. It was so much fun. My niece really liked singing.

Next, they took all of us to San Francisco for the day. We took a ferry boat ride around the Bay. They even asked us if we wanted to do the helicopter ride over the water. There was no way I was ever getting in a helicopter. We really had a good time in San Francisco and even rode those famous cable cars.

It was time for Ma to leave soon after our little trip to the Bay. I hated to see her leave because we were finally getting close to each other. No matter what the reason was I enjoyed the closeness.

Here I was back on my own again. Who knew what awaited me? Once more life without Ma!

CHAPTER 17

I started my life in Sacramento with a boyfriend. He said he was not my boyfriend, something that really didn't make any sense to me since we had plenty of sex, drugs and rock and roll. I gathered that all this free love is just what you did in California. He even introduced me to his Mom. So why weren't we a couple? Your guess is as good as mine.

He would visit me on a regular basis. My sister and her Man were usually at work and my niece was at the babysitters. So, we did all those things that young couples did. I'm not too proud of what we did now, but I must accept that it was what it was.

One night he even took me to a hotel. I didn't call my sister and tell her I wasn't coming home that night. I figured that she knew what was up. Looking back, I did think about calling her and probably should have, I just didn't. Anyway, the next day when I showed up at the house, my sister and her Man let me have it big time. It seems that she stayed up all night worrying about me.

My sister's Man didn't actually care; it was my sister worrying about me that made him mad. Well, I was surprised at my sister's reaction since my New York City sisters never worried about me. During the night, my sister called my boyfriend's Mom, who said that he was missing too. They put it together and figured out that we were together somewhere. Heck, I was twenty years old. I thought I was grown. When I got back to my sister's house her Man and I had one heck of a fight. To give you an idea of how bad our fight was, I actually ended up back in a psych ward. Here is how it went down.

Our big fight was all over the fact I stayed out all night with my so-called boyfriend. Somehow it seems that I must have interrupted their peaceful home. Give me a break. Once the yelling got to a certain volume, I started gathering my belongings from the closet, as if I had somewhere to go. At this point my sister's Man gathered me up in his arms and somehow put me in their car.

To the best of my memory I argued all the way to the hospital. I thought to myself, "I will get her for this," but what I said was truly awful. I accused my sister of being against black men. This is what I figured was her reason for taking me to a hospital. Since my Man was black, she didn't like him, mainly because her Man was white.

Today I realize that this made no sense at all. I really didn't care about her man's skin color; I just had to say something in my own defense. They were very mad at me. We argued and that trip to the hospital put me in the psych ward, just for being out all night.

Looking back, that almost seems funny. The sad part is I really went off in front of the doctors about this made up assumption on race. That was enough for them to decide to keep me in the psych ward. In those days, when I felt you are being unfair to me, I would go off on you with extremely hurtful words.

As far as I was concerned, they had started the fight, so I was going to end it on my terms. Well that didn't exactly turn out my way since I ended up spending two weeks in the psych ward at the Medical Center in Sacramento.

When I was in the hospital, my so call boyfriend came to visit me. He was told I was there because I had an abortion. What a lie. My sister's Man told my boyfriend that; I told him that was a lie. Well that was the end of that conversation and we never brought it up again.

Truth be told, the reasons I was there weren't too clear to me. I remember just going off on my sister and her man, because they attacked me for staying out all night. There was a yelling match and I was put in their car and brought to the hospital. They kept me because I was still yelling at them.

After my earlier experiences, I knew that I would never have another one of those nasty abortions. After all, it was those abortions that landed me in the psych ward in the first place. Deep down I knew something wasn't right with me thanks to two abortions.

I tried to explain this to my so-called boyfriend, but he didn't seem to be to concern about the real reason I was in the hospital. In the end, this experience really did change our relationship, since I now had to relocate from my sister's house.

My time in the Sacramento psych ward gave me no more insight into my emotional health than my earlier experiences in New York. I kept asking myself, "What's wrong with Joan," but no one was offering answers. I finally realized that it was up to me to pick myself up, dust myself off, and start all over. As cold as the world had left me feeling, I had to put all this on the back burner and move on.

After two long weeks in the psych ward, they finally let me go. When I got back to my sister's place, I spent the night at a neighbor's house. I was very glad to have befriended her earlier.

Needless to say, my sister's Man wanted me to leave their home. They were moving out of state. This news was delivered when I returned the next day from the neighbor's house. Given recent circumstances, I wasn't all that busted up about the idea. Don't get me wrong, I appreciated the three months that my sister put me up, but it was definitely time to move on.

CHAPTER 18

Here I am, back on my own with no job and no place to live. I lost the job I got when Ma was still here. It was an ok job working at a pretty well-known photography studio. I solicited customers for them, which was ok. Unfortunately, I must admit that my head was not really on the job and one day I just didn't want to go to work. I told them that I had "family problems," which was a lie. Like I said, I just didn't want to work that day. They fired me. At the time I was mad, but looking back I see that I was the problem.

So down I went to the welfare office. They put me on unemployment, which gave me a little over $100 a month to live on, something like $33 a week. Even in the 1970s there was no way I could live on that kind of money.

Back I went to the government, this time getting a general assistance check of something less than $200 a month. Even with both checks I was stuck in a roach infested, sleazy hotel in a bad part of town.

The welfare office actually put me there. I never saw my welfare checks since the hotel owner took them in exchange for room and board. The rent was about $81 a month and I got one meal a day that I could charge at their diner behind the rat trap hotel. I never saw the welfare check and actually signed the unemployment checks over to the hotel as well.

I ate once a day and got my entertainment from a community TV in the hotel lobby - Home Sweet Home. Now I bet you are wondering how I lived on less than $300.00 a month. Well it wasn't easy on just one meal a day.

My sister came to say goodbye before she left California. She wanted me to come with them, but I said no way! They were going to North or South Dakota and I knew that those places were even colder than New York City. I was in sunny California and planned to stay where it was warmer.

She cried and cried and then left. My sister and I never fully made up after the fight. It was basically her Man that wanted me out. My sister and I could have set some ground rules with each other, but he just wanted me out. Anyway, they were going to the cold Midwest and I was staying in the Golden State.

The conditions at that hotel were deplorable. It was basically a bunch of men on drugs or alcohol or both. My one meal a day was hardly sufficient, so I was hungry most of the time. Looking to combine safety and companionship, I befriended a gay guy. He and I would pan handle on the K Street Mall for nickels and dimes. He was on SSI and living in the hotel too. He didn't see his check either and we became good friends.

One of my other friends was a prostitute who worked the local streets for her pimp. She was a nice person who just couldn't get out of a horrible life. At one point I was hungry enough to think about prostituting myself. At the time I knew better than to get a pimp.

Being back on my own, I developed a plan. The first step of this plan was to get a boyfriend for protection. You are probably wondering what happened to my first California boyfriend. This was a strange relationship, even for me. I would see him once in a while, but always on his terms, and I do mean terms. There really wasn't any love there. This old boyfriend was really only interested in sex from me with no strings attached. I went along with it for a while because I had no one else. I was alone in California.

There I was, on my own in a flea bag hotel with two friends, a gay guy, and a prostitute. It may seem strange, but I really wasn't scared staying in that place by myself. Although I was already 20 years old, I looked much younger. I met a neighbor who I befriended. He was a nice guy who worked during the day, and when he came to the hotel at night, he wanted me to sleep in his room for my protection. He told me that he was afraid for me in that place.

I actually did sleep in his room. I know this sounds crazy, but no sex was involved. He actually wanted to protect me.

As with many parts of my transitory life, the day came when he was ready to move out. He told me that he was involved with a woman somewhere. She must have been special since he spoke of her often. After he left, I considered myself lucky to have known him. He was a little older than me and hardworking, decent guy. He offered, and actually provided, protection for me in that flea bag hotel. I was sorry to see him go.

Then one day my luck changed. I thought it was for the better, but that turned out not to be the case. I was in the hotel lobby watching TV when this guy came in. He was really cute. It was one of those things where young people just click and before you know it, we were laughing and smiling at each other. We started talking and laughing and got to know each other really quick. Maybe we got to know each other too quick.

That first night we met we spent the night together. He left his job. Which was out of town.

After our first night he ended up staying for good. This was fine with me since I probably did need the protection. Not that I was afraid of the hotel, but it could get scary sometimes.

Believe it or not, the owners of the hotel were pretty nice about my situation. I wasn't supposed to have overnight guests, but they overlooked my new roommate. Right away he became my Man. He had a little money from his time working collecting unemployment checks. Unfortunately, that didn't go all that far.

I put two meals a day on credit at the hotel diner, one for me and one for him. Then someone told me about a waitress job. I went and got the job and ended up supporting this boyfriend for a while. I made pretty good money with tips from the restaurant that I worked at and thought to myself that maybe this is how you keep a Man in California - support him. So, I kept that up for a while.

Next thing I knew the holidays were coming. There was no way I was going to spend Thanksgiving in that rat trap of a hotel. I ventured out of the K Street Mall area where I lived and saw a man cleaning outside of an apartment complex that actually looked pretty nice. I asked about the rent and he told me he had a furnished studio apartment for $105 a month. The apartment was very nice, with nice furniture. I couldn't believe my luck.

Sometimes you just don't understand people. I will never understand why that dirty rat of a boyfriend of mine wanted me to stay in that awful hotel with him. He knew rent was cheap in Sacramento. Even my sister knew rent in Sacramento was cheap and didn't tell me to look for another place. Amazing.

I filled out an application and credit check, which came back good. The deposit to move in was just $45, so move in I did. After realizing that he kept me in the dark about local rents, I wanted to leave the boyfriend where I found him. But I let him tag along. Well that should have been an obviously mistake. Let me go back a little in time and tell you how he became an even bigger rat.

Around the time I was living it that flea bag hotel, I started to prostitute my body. Yes, that is what I said. I must admit that it was my idea.

I came up with the idea because we were hungry, and I wanted to get out of that rat trap hotel. He was fine with the idea, of course. I got together with my prostitute friend and we would go to the bars and trick separately. This seemed to be working until I got arrested and spent a week in jail. It was a misdemeanor crime against me, so the judge let me out with a stern lecture to never return to his court again. Believe me, that was my intent.

After that experience, I got a waitress job in a local restaurant, a job that unfortunately lasted just a couple of months. You see I worked the graveyard shift and this male customer reached out and felt my behind. I don't take that from no man I don't know, and I cursed him out for putting hands on me. It wasn't long after that I lost that job. I can't say I missed the work, but I certainly did miss those tips.

There we were with no money and rent to pay. I decided it might be time to once again sell my body for money. As before, it was my idea, but that rat boyfriend was fine with the idea. He didn't want to work anyway, so when rent time came up, I hit the "hoe stroll" for rent money.

He was not technically my pimp, even though he wanted to be a pimp. He actually had the nerve to introduce me to a real prostitute who did want to be his "hoe." By this time, I was about done with him and thought this might actually be a good way to get rid of him.

They told me some BS story about why she wanted to work for him, and I told her I had a better idea. She should have him all for herself. Get him out of here. Take him with you. Unfortunately, they didn't want that kind of a plan. For some unknown reason, he wanted to stay with me. My paying the rent could have had something to do with that idea. Just my luck.

Soon after that mess he actually got a real job. My prostitution days had lasted six months, and it was the worst thing I ever did to my body, or my soul for that matter. I regretted that lifestyle for sure. My only excuse was that I only did it when the cupboards were empty and needed rent money.

Anyway, after two months of work he quit his job. That did it for me. I quit him. I was done with that loser for good. All together we were together a year and a half.

Looking back, this man had real problems. Unfortunately for him, he wasn't any good at it. He was too nice of a person. For example, he didn't pimp me or tell me what to do with my life, and that is what real pimps did. My friend the prostitute from the hotel had a real pimp. He controlled her like you cannot believe.

I wonder what happened to that crazy boyfriend, especially when I hear those old Teddy Pendergrass records. That was his favorite artist. I did run into him a few times after our breakup and he always claimed he loved me. I do hear he is still around, but haven't seen him.

CHAPTER 19

Picture this, it is the middle of 1980 and Sacramento, California was beautiful. But there I was alone. I might as well be alone given the losers I picked up. Let's see, there was that first boyfriend who didn't claim to be my boyfriend but certainly enjoyed all that sex, drugs, and rock and roll. Then there was the idiot at the sleaze-bag hotel that I supported by selling my body in between real jobs so that we could eat. He was a lazy bum. No wonder I was alone. You know what, I was glad of it.

I was working at the Mansion Inn in Sacramento as a maid. In some ways that was a great job. I actually met a very famous black country singer, who stayed at the hotel. Believe it or not, he said he would have spent the night with me, which would have cost him a pretty penny. Then there was Don Grady, he played the part of the eldest son Robbie on the television show My Three Sons. He gave me an autographed picture of himself, even though I didn't ask for it. I still have it to this day.

Going back to school sounded like a good idea to me. It wasn't easy since I worked during the day and went to school four nights a week. Even so, it was perfect!

Not knowing exactly what to take, I enrolled in a typing class. I didn't especially enjoy typing but for some reason I knew that this was a good idea. I also took a computer class. At the time I knew nothing about computers and to tell the truth, I still have trouble with computers even today.

I attended Sacramento City College. In some ways this was sort of a strange experience. I didn't really know what I wanted to take in college. Even though I had previously considered journalism, looking back I'm surprised that taking this direction never came to mind. To be honest, I got very little out of my college experience, but I went because I thought I should.

As for my social life, at this point I really didn't want one. I needed to find myself. I was a lost soul and besides, men were always more trouble than they were worth.

So, what went wrong? Well, at the moment the only friends that I had were a couple we will call Jack and Jill. They were held over friends from when I had that loser live-in boyfriend for a year and a half. They invited me over to their home, which was not very far from where I lived at the time. I should have known better, but they had a man at their home that they wanted me to meet. I was really mad, and I gave him the cold shoulder the whole night. I was not interested at all!!! Even though he was a pretty nice-looking guy, no way!!

There was no doubt about it. I needed a break from the last loser I saddled myself with. You remember, the one that didn't mind me prostituting my body so I could keep a roof over his head and food in his belly - that loser.

Jill actually understood why I gave her friend the cold shoulder and he left earlier than expected. Jill tried to explain to her man Jack why I gave him the cold shoulder, but Jack was a horrible person himself. Oh, did he make me mad that night. He actually thought he was doing me a favor. Can you believe that? No thank you!!!

There I was at City College, not knowing exactly why I was going there. I felt as if somehow everything would eventually just fall in place. I just kept on going. One thing I did know was that if you didn't get an education in this country, you are doomed.

You are not going to guess who I ran into while going the City College - the guy my friends had tried to hook me up with. Turns out he took the same bus that I took on my way home from school at night. I still wasn't interested in him until he told me he was from, East Coast. All of a sudden, he had one good thing going for him, he wasn't from California. I was totally done with these California men.

Boy was he charming. We would spend the weekends together. Yes, just like that. It moved really fast. We both bought bikes and would go bike riding. It was great fun. He tried roller skating with me, but the skates were too fast for me. So that didn't work out.

Then one day he proposed to me. No, not marriage, he wanted to get an apartment together, so we could share expenses and save money. At first, I really didn't like the idea, but he kept harping on it.

By this time, I had finished my first year at City College and believe it or not, I got all A's and B's. You would think that this level of success would encourage me to stay in school, and you would be wrong. I decided to leave City College and enroll in a business college, so I found one and signed up for a secretarial course. The truth of the matter is that this charming new boyfriend was messing with my concentration at City College.

His harping finally paid off and by the time I entered the business school we had moved in with each other. We had a nice little apartment. He picked the apartment out and even arranged for us to be the apartment managers. That saved a bunch of rent money. To this day I still don't know how he managed to make us the managers. At the moment, I thought that the worst part of the deal was that I had to give up my cat.

So, life was perfect, right? WRONG! On our first night in the apartment this "knight and shining armor" of mine became more like Dr. Jekyll and Mister Hyde. He showed a completely different side of himself and I knew from the first night I had made a mistake.

He was studying in the bedroom and I fell asleep watching the TV in the living room. All of a sudden, I woke up to him yelling at me; something about coming to bed. I knew at that very moment that this was another side of him I didn't like. It was clear that he was a mean person.

I really didn't want to move in with him in the first place, but because of his persistence in asking I did. But to wake up to his yelling at me on the first night we were in the apartment together was a strange thing that left a bad taste in my mouth. I knew than something was wrong with him.

Despite his new attitude, I figured it was best to play it cool until I could get out. During this time, my sister Gail from New York came to visit us. Now Gail knew something was wrong and told me to get out as soon as I could, and I told her I would.

Gail stayed with us for a week. When it was time for her to leave, she went into my boyfriend's bedroom, where he was studying. When she came out, we walked outside to wait for the shuttle van that was going to take her to the airport. While we were waiting, I asked Gail what she said to him. She leaned in and said, "I told him that if he hurt my sister, I was going to kill you." You may think that is pretty bold, but that is how Gail was. She didn't play and you always knew she meant it.

Some of the things my Jekyll/Hyde boyfriend did to me were very strange. In the four short months I lived with him he made my life very miserable.

As I mentioned, we were the apartment managers, so we had to interact with lots of people. Well Jekyll/Hyde accused me of sleeping with every Tom, Dick and Harry that crossed our path. I sold Avon on the side for extra money, but he accused me of sleeping with my customers. He was obviously not bright enough to realize that my Avon customers were all women. Although at the time I did have one very old man who bought Avon for his girlfriend. He had to be close to ninety years old. I thought it was even cute he had a girlfriend. The old man called me for an order, and I guess that set him off. You could tell he was old by his voice on the phone. That nut Jekyll/Hyde still thought I was sleeping with him.

Some of our neighbors were male and he accused me of sleeping with some of them. One day we stayed in the apartment all day and he wouldn't let me answer the front door to anyone who knocked. Another time he cornered me in the bathroom and said, "If you say something, I am gonna knock you thru that wall."

Meanwhile I was saving my money to get out of there and get out I did. Unfortunately, he found me. Seems the moving boxes in the garbage cans gave me away. He figured out that I was going back to where I came from and that made me too easy to find.

Downtown Sacramento is not that big to begin with so Jekyll/Hyde figured I would return to the area I came from. He was right. I did go back to my old area. All he had to do was go around to the different apartment complexes owned by the State and check the garbage dumpsters. When he found my boxes that way, he knew which apartment I lived in. No brainer for him. As a matter of fact, I knew he could find me that way.

For all his faults, Jekyll/Hyde was a real charmer, but then I was also rather young and impressionable. He poured on the charms and before I knew it, I had spent the night with him at our old apartment that we had together. What a big mistake on my part. What was I thinking?

The next morning, he kicked me out the front door, butt naked! Thank God none of the neighbors saw me. It was early in the morning and they were still sleeping. Needless to say, I was finished with that crazy man for sure. I managed to put on my clothes outside the apartment and walked home. That was it - goodbye NUT!!!

CHAPTER 20

Well, I escaped the clutches of Dr. Jekyll and Mister Hyde, which left me once again alone in Sacramento.

Like most people, I'd rather be alone than dead. I will forever believe that man wanted to do me harm. Even so, I have always felt that Dr. Jekyll and Mister Hyde didn't do me harm because of what my sister Gail told him. As you probably remember, Gail told him that she would kill him if he ever hurt her sister, meaning me. Knowing Gail, she meant it. To tell you the truth, I believe that is why she visited me in the first place, she wanted to make sure I was safe. Gail always did look after me, even though she was my younger sister.

Let me tell you about life back on my own. At the time I was working regularly and attending MTI Business College. I made some new friends, but still felt the loneliness at times. Of the friends I made at this time, one has remained a good friend even to this day. Mind you, that was over thirty years ago.

I knew that I needed more education if I wanted to get a better job. At the time I was a maid at several of the hotels in the Sacramento area. I really wanted something better for myself, although I didn't like secretarial work. Go figure that out.

There were actually several different reasons I didn't want secretarial work. First of all, my hands would get painful if I typed very long. Add to that the thought of a boss chasing me around the office and I was totally turned off to the idea. Even so, I did consider working in a big office pool situation with a lot of secretaries. I just didn't enjoy the work as much.

Even with all these misgivings, I didn't know what else to do in my life. I thought business would be a good career for me. At least I could make some decent money. Believe it or not, I actually liked my maid job. There was no stress and I was able to work alone. The day went by fast, which was a real plus for me.

While in school I took out a student loan, which really came in handy when I lost my job. I was working at one of the local hotels and when business dropped, they laid me off. There was little or no work as a hotel maid in Sacramento at the time mostly because this was the Christmas season and there weren't many people coming to town.

No problem, I was young and foolish, so I decided to take my Student loan money and visit my family in New York City. The loan was about $1,500 which, at the time, was a lot of money. It took me several years to pay it back, but I did pay it back.

It was Christmas, 1980 and I hadn't seen my New York family in nearly three years. Now most of my California friends and acquaintances figured I was from New York City. If you asked them, they would tell you that I had an accent. When I would tell them that I was in Sacramento living on my own without family, they were always surprised. This was not typically the way a young girl in the 1980s lived.

I never thought it was so strange. After all, it's a free country. Right?

I knew I was going to be broke when I got home from visiting my family. That was a little scary, but I figured I would deal with that when I got back - the thinking of a young person, no doubt.

First, I got a round trip airline ticket to New York City. That cost me $200. I knew that while I was in New York I would take some time and go to Alabama to visit my parents, so I inquired about bus fare south. That meant a Greyhound Bus ride and another round-trip ticket to buy. Back then it didn't cost that much to ride the bus, but it did take a lot of time. The ride alone down and back took about 24 hours. All in all, the total length of my Christmas trip home was two weeks.

New York was fun but freezing. In a very short time, I realized that this was one of the reasons I left. The place was just too darn cold! Even so, I had a good time with my friends and family. I even bought them Christmas presents. As you may remember, to help make ends meet I sold the product Avon products on the side. Everyone, all my friends and family, got Avon products from me for Christmas.

When I got off that plane in New York City I looked good, even if I say so myself. You don't have to believe me, that is what they all said. I had on a full-length leather coat that I bought from one of my school mates. I guess she felt she didn't need the coat in California. I was sharp and my hair was long and in a nice hair style. I would never have said it to them directly, but the two sisters that picked me up from the airport didn't look half as good as I did. To me it seemed as if New York City had not been all that kind to them. But heck, I was back home and happy to be there.

Everybody was busy with their lives, but most weren't doing as well as I would expect. New York City was then and is today a hard town on your pocketbook. It is an expensive place to live. I've often wondered how Ma and Daddy could have afforded living there.

My sisters were working hard just to keep a roof over their heads. They were also going to college and all the stress of school, work and life in New York City managed to show up in the form of their looks. Don't get me wrong, I love my sisters, but their age was starting to catch up with them. They just didn't look the same. At least not the way I remembered them.

But I was here to have some fun and fun I had. Before I knew it, it was time to head south to Alabama to visit my parents. The ride to Alabama took 24 hours. I slept most of the way there and back, which helped to pass the time. My parents were very well and of the same mind when it came to me. Not surprising, they wanted me to stay in Alabama. For some reason, my parents didn't want me to grow up.

By now this California Girl was not having any part of that idea. I was not going to stay in those woods with nothing fun to do and having my parents there to watch my every step.

I had tasted life on my own and I loved it. I had a nice visit with them, and before I knew it, it was time to head back to New York and to fly back to Sacramento.

My best friend gave me a ride to the airport, but she was late picking me up. It was a good thing I was young and healthy because I had to run through the airport to catch my plane. I got there just in the nick of time. A minute more and they would probably have left without me.

The trip back to Sacramento was no fun at all. I was sick as a dog. I must have caught the flu or something, or maybe it was a little too much party. The plane was a DC10, which is a huge airplane, and fortunately it was a non-stop flight from New York City to San Francisco. To my surprise, the plane was actually pretty empty, giving me the chance to lay down in a row of seats and cough my way home. I can't imagine the other passengers were all too happy about that.

Once I got home to Sacramento, and Sacramento was now my home, I decided that this was probably going to be my last trip to New York City in the winter. For one thing, the weather is just too darn cold. I'd become a California girl who wasn't going to put up with that ice and snow.

The second reason was the cost of everything. No matter how hard you work, it just seemed impossible to get ahead. The rent is too high and what you get is not very cozy and nice. Eventually most of my friends left New York City because of the cost of living. At least you get a decent place to live in California without the roaches as your roommates. I was glad to be back in California.

CHAPTER 21

Here I am back in Sacramento! This time I can truly call it "home sweet home." By now I knew that I wasn't ever returning to the East Coast or the South to live again - visit yes, live there, no.

My reasons were actually pretty straight forward. I now lived pretty comfortably in Sacramento. Except for the loneliness, I actually lived pretty well. I had a nice studio apartment; the rent was $130 a month. I knew I could make that kind of money from somewhere, even if I had to work night and day. You see my father had taught me to work hard.

One thing I had learned by then was that people will try to take advantage of you, especially when they find out you have no family around. That was no problem for me because I learned early on not to trust people outside the family. This made it hard for someone to take advantage of me. You might say I had a defense mechanism built inside me all the time. Gail and I, that's my closest sister, had a saying when we were growing up; "If you are not my sister, you are a bitch." That said, we both had lots of friends, but they never knew we felt like that. It was our little secret.

I am back in Sacramento with no money and no job. I had been laid off from the hotel for the winter months. I planned on going back after the slow season was over.

There was a funny story about that job. I was working as a housekeeper for a hotel in West Sacramento called The El Rancho Hotel. You will never guess who stayed there - my idol, Lucille Ball! No one told me she was staying in the hotel. I just saw her Rolls Royce leaving the hotel one day and asked who it was. That is when a friend told me it was Lucille Ball in the Rolls Royce.

I was really mad that I had missed meeting her. I would have asked her if I could be her personal maid. If she had said yes, I would have dropped everything and got in that limo that very moment. And I do believe there was a good chance she would have said yes. Lucille Ball was in town because her son was in a play at a local theater called The Music Circus in downtown Sacramento. Well what a letdown I had that day.

As far as my personal life went, I was alone again and glad of it. "Dr. Jekyll and Mister Hyde" was fresh in my mind. He had found out where I lived by looking for my boxes in the garbage dumpsters in the area where I moved to. What a freak. He figured I would go back to the area I had lived before, and he was right.

One day he knocked on my door; that was very scary. I wouldn't have anything to do with him. As far as I was concerned, he was a real nut. Eventually he left Sacramento. Finished school and the last I heard of him he moved back to the East Coast. At that point, I didn't care how lonely I got. I never wanted to see him again. At one point he even had the nerve to propose marriage to me. What a joke!

Before he left Sacramento, I actually invited him to my 23rd birthday party. To tell the truth, I'm not really sure why I invited him other than the fact I was very lonely. He actually came but was sick that night and didn't stay very long. There's no telling what he would have done if he had stayed.

Since I love parties, I actually threw this one for myself. The party was a success. Everyone had a lot of fun. We danced all night. Smoked and drank. I made lasagna. Everyone had a good time.

Well after the party loneliness set in again. It was depressing always being alone. But that was my life at that time. I had no family and I didn't know my friends very well. But they were good friends, I thought. To this day I only keep up with one of the persons that were at my party. I try not to think about it too much. So, I kept myself busy as I possibly could have. I was in school and tried to work too. But let's face it I was in a foreign land trying to fit in. I kept asking myself if such a nice place to live was worth the loneliness. Well I guess it was, since I'm still here in Sacramento; and I'm lonely again!

CHAPTER 22

Along came another lonely weekend, so I decided to go to treat myself to dinner at my favorite restaurant in Old Sacramento, a pizza parlor called Straw Hat Pizza. From my apartment the restaurant was a short walk through Capitol Park, something I had done numerous times before. What started out as a typical walk turned into something wonderful.

As I crossed the park, a man came walking toward me. Immediately my defense mechanism went up. I thought, "Oh no, here comes a man who will probably approach me." By then I was totally done with Sacramento men, that was for sure. They were so vulgar in their attempt to get your attention. They only wanted one thing, sex, and then they wanted the woman to take care of them. How lazy can you get? At least that was my opinion of Sacramento men at that time.

From a few feet away he smiled at me. He had a really nice smile! Then he asked me for a match. In those days I smoked cigarettes, so I gave him a match. He introduced himself and asked me my name. We exchanged that much and then he said the magic word, "I'm from New York - The Bronx." He had my attention.

He told me he was working a concert that night and asked if I would like to see the Bar Kays in concert. The Bar Kays were a 1960s R & B group out of Memphis. Once he showed me his backstage passes, I figured it was for real.

When he asked me where I was going, I told him I was heading to Straw Hat Pizza to get something to eat. He asked if he could go with me to the pizza parlor so off we went together on a cloudy afternoon in February 1981. What amaze me was that it was not even cold out. All you needed was a light jacket. Remember I was born on the coldest day of the year in New York City. Not bad for a change.

I found myself comfortable talking with him right away. Here I was, telling him my problems, my likes and dislikes, and we discovered that we had a lot in common. I think mostly because we were both from New York City, we seemed to have an easy time talking to each other. How refreshing it is, I thought, to have someone to talk to.

Once we got to the restaurant, I ordered my all-you-can-eat salad bar and he ordered a piazza. He offered to pay and pulled out a big wad of money to pay for the food and drink. I thought it was amazing that he had a lot of money on him. He actually did have a job and that made him even more interesting.

He put the money back in his jacket pocket and we sat down. At this point he did something I thought was really strange. He took off his jacket, with the money in it, and set it down on his chair as he headed to restroom. This seemed really strange because he didn't know me at all, yet he trusted me with all his money. "Is this a test?" I asked myself.

Well, I wasn't a thief, but a thief would have taken his money and run. After all, any thief would have reasoned that he didn't know the town and headed for the door with jacket and cash in hand. But of course, he came out of the restroom and there I was, still there. We continued our conversations and it was refreshing to talk to someone who was on the same page as me.

We finished eating and headed toward my apartment. I kept thinking to myself, "What am I going to wear to the concert." I decided on my white Capri pants and the new blouse that my sister had given me for Christmas. Perfect!

On the way there I asked him if he could iron my pants because I hate ironing. I really did. Back home in New York my Mom made me iron everything when I was a little girl. But what really turned me off about ironing was having to iron my fathers' boxer shorts. Why in the name of heaven did I have to iron his underwear? Well that's another subject. My new friend didn't seem to mind ironing my pants, and he actually did a good job. So off we went to the concert. He even held my hand. Oh boy, no one ever did that in Sacramento before. I felt very special.

The concert was hilarious. As it turned out, we just had backstage passes, not seats in the auditorium. So, we went around looking for two empty seats together. We would find seats, but as soon as we would get settled the usher would come around and kick us out of those seats. Unfortunately for us, it was a full house.

We would laugh every time we got kicked out of the seats and it turned into a game after a while. The concert was loud, and, in my opinion, the Bar Kays did not give a good performance. They were just loud. They only had one hit song that I liked anyway. My escort had the same feelings I did about the band, he didn't like them either in concert, so after the third time we got kicked out of seats we decided to leave.

By now it was about eleven o'clock at night and we were both hungry. We set out looking for a restaurant, which was no easy task in 1981 Sacramento. Downtown Sacramento pretty much rolled up the sidewalks at six o'clock each night.

We finally found a restaurant on 16th Street, not far from the auditorium. It was a nasty place, but we were hungry, so we sat down. The food was not good at all, but we talked the whole time we were together. I told him about my life in Sacramento. He thought it was a nice place to live. I told him I barely had any friends. I told him about the birthday party that I threw for myself. And I told him about "Dr. Jekyll and Mister Hyde." He listened intently. We talked in the restaurant and on the way back to my apartment. Then he asked me if I knew of a store that might be open.

The only place I knew of was a 24-hour drug store, an all-nighter as we called them. He wanted to walk there, which was fine with me. I knew he was a true New Yorker when I saw how he didn't mind walking. Walking was something else we both had in common.

On the way to the drug store he asked me if he could spend the night with me and I thought, "Oh boy, here it comes." I assumed he wanted to have sex with me.

I said "no" but when he heard my reason, he said he just didn't want to go to a hotel and was looking for a place to sleep. I explained to him if he spent the night in my apartment there would be no hanky and definitely no panky. Just sleep. He said that was fine, of course.

Truth be told, I didn't actually trust him, and I figured I should get some cream for my birth control device. I needed to be prepared, just in case. No way was I going to get pregnant by this stranger.

We arrived at the drug store and he asked me if I wanted anything. I did want that cream but was too embarrassed to ask for some. To my surprise, he picked up a pint of Johnnie Walker Red. By the time we reached my apartment, his pint was gone. I thought this was a red flag if I ever saw one. The funny thing was that it didn't change him. He never really appeared to get drunk. So, I dismissed it. He carried on in conversation as if he never had a drink. But that night was going to change my whole life.

CHAPTER 23

Needless to say, I was young and didn't know very much. The reason I say that is that I just invited a stranger to spend the night with me, in my bed, because he didn't want to go to a hotel. Of course, I also stipulated no hanky-panky as rule number One, which he agreed to. At the time, I thought this was a good idea on my part, since I had no birth control available. Like I said, young and dumb.

You may remember that I had gone without birth control two times before, and each of those two times I ended up getting an abortion. I was not doing that again. So, birth control was very important to me. On top of that, I didn't even know him!!!

So off we went to my apartment. Now here is a real shock, since he had been drinking, he actually did want to have sex. I just knew that this was a bad idea because I was sure that I would get pregnant. After all, I was expecting "Mister Monthly" in two weeks.

I'm sure it is no surprise that he didn't just roll over and go to sleep. I told him I had no protection and that he had to pull out in time. You know that he said that was fine, but in the moment such promises are quickly forgotten. His manhood was all over me. I gave him a good cursing out and told him I was sure he had just made me pregnant. After all, I know my body and I was very fertile. This is the third time I didn't have birth control when having sex. There was nothing for me to do but get cleaned up and go to sleep and hope for the best; he did the same.

Now who is to blame? I was for letting him in my bed in the first place. After all, he was a drunk young man with sex on his brain. He even had this surprise look on his face when I yelled at him for not pulling out in time. Now that I think of it, he was drunk and probably didn't know what was going on. I'm not making excuses for him; it's just that he had such a strange look on his face. I think my yelling snapped him back to reality.

By the next day I had calmed down, at least a little. I told him I was pregnant. His brilliant comment was that he didn't think I was pregnant so let's go get some birth control for tonight. Can you believe this man? Even so, I was all for that idea just in case by some miracle I wasn't pregnant.

We actually got along great, despite my concerns, and he ended up spending a week with me. It was very nice. We used birth control and enjoyed each other's company. But I knew it was too late for the birth control.

Then came the day when he had to leave. It was time for him to go back to work. As part of his job he traveled with various entertainers from city to city, state to state. I knew it was going to be hard to get in touch with him, so he gave me his parents' phone number on the east coast and off to work he went.

For the next few weeks I waited and waited for "Mister Monthly" to come, but he never arrived. I was scared and all that I could think about was the fact that I was going to have a baby.

I called the number he gave me and much to my surprise he was at his parents' house. I told him about no monthly visitor but he just laughed and said, "That's right, I "_____ you." How vulgar I thought.

It was clear that this fool was not going to be of much help. Fortunately, I became friends with his sister. He would continue to work with traveling entertainers, and I remained in the business college. I had about four months to go before I graduated.

So, I went to school and my belly grew. I knew no one was going to hire me after I finished school because I was with child, which turned out to be the case. After finishing school, I ended up back on welfare. I kept asking myself what I was going to do. I was not ready to be a Mom. I was alone without family. Boy did I want that man to come back to Sacramento. His usual excuse was that he had to work and there wasn't work for him in Sacramento.

CHAPTER 24

I didn't see that man again till I was six months pregnant. By that time a friend of mine had convinced me to visit a friend of hers. This friend of hers was a Jehovah's Witness. It took a long time for me to agree to have a visit from a Jehovah's Witness in my home.

The reason it took so long for me to agree for a Jehovah's Witness to visit me is summed up in one or two words. Hate and prejudice. This hate and prejudice didn't come on its own, inside of me, I had help. My parents displayed a hatred for Jehovah's Witnesses all my childhood life. Never answer the door if they were ringing the bell. My parents made it clear they hated Jehovah's Witnesses. And they rang our doorbell until someone would come to the door. So naturally when my friend and work mate told me she found the true religion and told me it was the Jehovah's Witnesses I particularly got sick to my stomach. No way was I going to let a Jehovah's Witness in my home.

I was just a couple of months pregnant, but by then I knew I needed a bigger place to live. I was living in a studio apartment made for just one person. I looked across the hall from me and I saw a empty spacious one-bedroom apartment. My first thought was, "That place is mines."

So, I applied for the spacious one bedroom across the hall from me. The rent was $179.00 a month. I was collecting $400.00 and something a month on welfare, plus food stamps so I figured I could budget that money just fine. I moved across the hall to a spacious one-bedroom apartment.

It may have been a bigger place to live, but I was so lonely while I was with child that it was almost unbearable. So, after a month of turning my friend down I finally said ok and let her friend come to visit. It turned out to be a very good visit. One that was a turning point in my life.

When the day came for my visit from the Jehovah's Witnesses, I had a big attitude about this visit. My parents instilled in me a big dislike for the Witnesses. When my friend brought Sally over for a visit, I was nasty toward her. I just knew I was going to end up kicking her out.

Sally started the conversation saying that she had heard I had a few questions."Oh Yeah," I said. My first question was why the Witnesses didn't celebrate Christmas. Sally told me that it was my choice if I wanted to celebrate Christmas. I thought that was a pretty good answer, so I started to listen.

As a result of this visit I began studying the bible in my home at least once a week. But what really made me study was the first paragraph of this book she shared with me. It was something I always wanted to hear. This book was called "The Truth That Leads to Eternal Life." Some people call this book the 'Blue Bombshell' because of its color.

The first paragraph was so profound to me. It asked a series of questions like, "Do you want to live in peace and happiness?" Well h--- yeah, I thought to myself. I wanted to know, "Do you desire good health and long life for yourself and loved ones?" "Do you long to see wickedness and suffering end?"

I knew immediately that this was something I had been looking for all my life.

My new friend, the Jehovah's Witness, and I began to read this book together. First, she would read a paragraph then I would read the next paragraph. After a while, she wanted to know if I would like to continue to study and I said yes. She asked if I would like to go to a meeting that Sunday and I again said I would. She promised to pick me up and guess what, she was good to her word. I had nothing else to do but sit and wait for my baby to come so I studied each week and went to the meetings on Sunday. I was learning what the bible says from the meetings and from my reading. It made sense to me.

CHAPTER 25

One day, much to my surprise, the father of my unborn child, Buck, showed up at my door. I was going into my sixth month of pregnancy now and he was working on the Rick James concert scheduled in Sacramento. I was in the middle of my bible study when he showed up. I was so glad to see him. We spent a week together. I was so happy during that week. But then he had to leave on the road again.

During that short week we enjoyed each other. We had a lot in common. It was as if he was a glove and I was the hand that fit the glove. An experience like that only came around once in my lifetime. Too bad it didn't last.

After he left, I continued to study the Bible and I was learning a great deal. My Bible study also taught me how to be a better Mom. As you might suspect, I did not have a clue about raising a child. The Bible saved me. It helped me grow up. I learned a little more every time I studied. This was very important to me since it certainly looked like I was going to be a single Mom. Even so, the loneliness was awful as I read the Bible to my unborn child.

I had a baby shower and got everything I needed for a newborn baby. The baby shower was at my home. My best friend at that time, who I had met on a past job, helped put the shower together. My friends from the Business College also came as did one of my neighbors and the girl that introduced me to the Jehovah's Witnesses. A lot of people came to help relieve my loneliness. My baby got everything a baby needed. Some friends couldn't make it, but they sent the gifts. Even two guys showed up. I never totally knew why they showed up but suspected it was to see all the girls.

CHAPTER 26

Then it was time to have my baby. A good friend of mine picked me up I stayed at her house until it was time to go to the hospital. My baby boy took 38 hours to arrive. The labor was not hard except for the last four hours. What an experience. No drugs, natural childbirth. 8 pounds 3 oz.

My son was the best thing that ever happened to me! No Dad to help me, but oh well!

Well there I was in Sacramento having a baby. I was all alone without any family to help me. Not even the baby's father!

The pitiful thing is I had just met this man. He was passing through Sacramento and stayed with me for a few days. For all I knew he could have been married.

I liked what I was learning from the Jehovah's Witness lady. She never judged me or asked me any personal questions. She became a good friend to me. I believed what I was learning, and this is what helped me to become a better person. I especially needed to become a good Mom. For I didn't have a clue.

Finally, my son came. Boy what a big baby. He had an "old" look about himself. Maybe because I use to talk to him. There was no one else to talk to. I also read the bible stories to him. I always told him, "just you and me." I was so happy he was a boy. I didn't want a girl, the reason for that is because I had seven sisters. Enough with the women. When I was growing up, I wished I had brothers instead of sisters.

It took my son 38 hours to be born. But when he was finally coming out, I was so happy! To this day I know that he was the next to the best thing that ever happened to me - studying the bible and getting to know God was the best thing that happened to me.

I had something to share with my son. I had a lot to teach him so he can grow up to be a fine citizen.

While I was in labor, if I wanted the labor pains to stop, I would call his name and tell him to stop the contractions and he would do so. We had bonded before he was even born. It must have been all that reading I did out loud so he could hear it also. I also told him how I felt about being alone. I told him it was just going to be me and him. My son heard me and knew me before he was even born. I had no one else to talk to. Of course, I bugged a couple of my old school mates every now and then on the phone. But they had their own lives to tend to. And there was my son's god mother, I worked with her on the first real job I got in Sacramento. Her name was Carrie, We lost contact years ago. But my son did meet her.

So finally, after being in labor so long it was time for my Dr to come to my aid. Dr Steven Thorn. I was in love with my Dr. He told me he was going to let a student do the delivery. I was to the point where who cared who delivered the baby. I wanted him out.

So, he says don't push Joan. What! I thought, "Are you crazy?" I wanted the baby OUT! So, I ignored him and I pushed really hard. He came out. But he tore me. Well he should have told me why I should not pushed. But he didn't and I wasn't asking any questions at that particular time. I needed to push so I did.

Unfortunately, I needed stitches. Three or four to be exact. The student person numbed me down there and stitched me up. Well the numbness didn't work. I felt each stitch. It was the worst part. Dr Thorn says oh please Joan you haven't said anything up until now. Well I was able to take the labor pains, but the stitches were unbearable.

Go figure!!

There he was, not saying a word just looking at me. I was shocked because I really didn't know what he was going to look like. I just looked at him. Dr Thorn said' you can touch him Joan'. So, I touched his leg. Remember he was 8 pounds 3ounces. I looked at him in shock because he was so big. How did he come out of me? I was so happy!

CHAPTER 27

After my son was born, I did not go home right away. I spent two days at my best friend Carrie's home. I had a ball with her family. We laughed and had a good time. My son was very quiet, he seemed so content. Maybe it was because I had a stress-free pregnancy. Remember, I was alone for the most part of my pregnancy.

After two days it was time to go home alone with my son. My milk came in during those two days at Carrie's house. It was very painful, but worth it. I could feed my baby with nutritional food.

I have to admit I was a little scared to go home by myself with my son. Oh well my mother was on her way. My mother was great. She was going to travel on a bus all the way from Alabama to California to help me out. This made me feel a lot better about my being alone.

I had all kinds of mixed feelings about my mother's visit bubbling up inside of me. First, I put my mother way up on a pedestal. If anyone was going to heaven she was going for sure. Not me, I had a baby out of wedlock. This made me feel uncomfortable.

There was a measure of guilt growing within me knowing that I had to face my mother. She was a virgin when she married. She had ten children with one man - my father. Mom never explained the "birds and the bees" to me so it's no wonder I ended up doing the things I did. I had to copy the world as I saw it because that's all I knew. Needless to say, I was embarrassed to have a baby out of wedlock. I just knew I wasn't going to do it again.

By the time Momma got to California I was not sleeping. This was not good. My embarrassment about the fact of being an unwed mother grew but at the same time I wanted to share with my newfound faith with my mother. I was convinced it was the true religion. I wasn't baptized at the time, but I just knew my mother would love the truths I found in the Bible. After all, my mother was a very religious person and she definitely believed in the Bible. All these thoughts kept running thru my mind. Was I being a hypocrite?

Momma looked well when she arrived, and I was happy to see her. I was so happy to see her that I cried on her safe arrival. I was shamed and happy at the same time. You see I viewed my mother as pure and good and at the time didn't think too much of myself. My mother was a virgin when she married my Dad. I really wanted to live like that myself, but who was going to marry me? No one did so far.

My mother wanted to know right off the bat if I wanted her to take my baby back to Alabama with her. Fortunately, she could see I had a nice place to live and my son had more than enough clothes to wear, mostly thanks to the people I knew. He also had a cradle, a swing set, and everything he needed. Of course, I said no to her question. One of my sisters called and asked Momma what I needed for the baby,

I heard her say, he doesn't need anything. That made me feel good.

One of my first thoughts was to share my findings in the bible with my mother. I showed her God's name in the Bible - Psalms 83:18. I truly believed that she would get this; she is a bible person. She didn't appreciate my newfound religion. So instead of me backing off, I doubled down. I really wanted to save my mother.

I was more confused and not sleeping at all. The guilt in me drove me a little nuts. I was having a nervous breakdown in front of my mother.

The guilt I was feeling about my situation effected my sleep. My thoughts became distorted while Momma was with me. I became irrational and started treating Momma badly. The problem was she couldn't see the bible the way I was seeing the bible. This and everything else just didn't mix well. Meaning, I had a nervous breakdown with her in the house with me.

I was impossible to live with. What did Momma do? She again suggested taking my son away from me and I told her no way. So, she started to plan her early exit. I was out of my mind at the time, so Momma left one morning.

What a disaster. I drove her away. Deep down I wanted her to stay. I was not myself at all, so I guess it was best she cut her visit short. Believe me, I didn't plan it to be that way but as soon as she left, I collapsed and went to sleep.

Then the phone that hardly ever rang, rang. My sisters were mad at me. I didn't blame them. I really couldn't explain it. But as I looked back on it, I set myself up for another nervous breakdown. It had nothing to do with my son. He was the best thing that happened to me. Well the second-best thing. My newfound religion was the best thing that ever happened to me.

I was not aware of what was wrong with me. The sleep I got right after Momma left was a big break for my mixed-up feelings. I started to come back to reality after that sleep. I knew I had to take care of my baby alone, so I got right down to business. Before

I knew it my son and I were in a marvelous routine. No stress from the outside world. It was beautiful, just him and me.

One reason momma left me was she knew I had everything I needed to take care of my son. We were lacking nothing at all. At the time I didn't view it this way, but my God really blessed me with everything I needed to take care of my healthy baby boy.

I love my mother dearly. Now I realize that I was getting sick before she arrived and never meant to hurt her.

CHAPTER 28

After Momma left, I got into real good routine. It was all peaceful and we got into a real good schedule. Everything was going quite well. I treated my son like the gift he was.

Soon it was time to go to his first doctor appointment. My son was very healthy, and he had a good checkup. My loneliness was not overpowering me like it did before. I still looked for my son's father to join us.

I heard he was going to be in San Francisco. He was supposed to come to Sacramento. He was working with the entertainer "Prince." Prince was to appear in San Francisco. Buck, my son's father. never showed up in Sacramento. I was very hurt he didn't want to see his son. As you might guess, I had feelings for him. Buck and I had gotten along so well together. I didn't understand. What the problem was. I had to move on, but I still thought about him all the time.

My loneliness was not as bad as it was before. Then there was Christmas. What an issue. I knew I should not celebrate Christmas, because my faith told me that was a pagan holiday, but I wanted to do it one more time. So, I had a little tree and had a present for my son under the tree.

After I left their home I walked back to my empty house and had a nervous breakdown. I shut myself in the house. I was so depressed about not having a whole family. Don't get me wrong, this had nothing to do with my son. It was me and this problem that I had and never knew what it was. So, I just thought I was crazy. I don't know how I took care of my son the next few days. But eventually I came out of it. I didn't hurt my son I just did what I normally did for him and I was super depressed. So, you see, celebrating that holiday one more time didn't do me any good.

New Years was no better. I started to question my newfound faith. I remember calling one of my sisters at New Years and said something about the Jehovah's Witnesses. She must have asked me how the studying made me feel. I told her good, so she said to continue if it made me feel good. After that talk with her I did continue my studies and began to teach my son. I found joy in doing so. I grew stronger in my convictions of what the truth is. And I saw the blessings coming my way. I treated my son as a gift from God. And I just wanted it to be just the two of us.

I continued my study of the bible and tried to live by what I was learning. It was very beneficial for me. I was a good Mom. I loved my baby so much. I didn't work for his first year on earth.

I felt the blessings and I continued to treat my son as the gift he was. His father never came to see him. That was hard to get over. It is what it is.

CHAPTER 29

What a screw up! After all, things were going great for me and my son. So why did I make the biggest screw up of my life? There is only one thing I achieved out of this screw up, and it is this book.

Things were going too well I guess, so I had to screw up. Life was good and I was grounding myself as a single Mom. I had Jehovah God and my son. My son was getting big and I was getting even more religious.

We went to the meetings at the Kingdom Hall of Jehovah's Witnesses. We went for walks every day, to the K Street Mall downtown Sacramento. Things were good. I had a wonderful schedule. A peaceful and fulfilling life. No stress. My son seemed like the best baby in the world. He was so good that my neighbors accused me of not having a baby in my house. You see my son never cried. He was very content. He did cry at bedtime, eight o'clock every night. He didn't want to go to bed.

All my needs were met, and that meant all of my son's needs were met as well. We were on welfare, but I budget the small amount of funds very well. My rent was only $179. We had a big one-bedroom apartment and I lived off of less than $500.00 a month plus food stamps. We were happy. So, what was the big screw up!!!

There was a family that came from NY to live with one of my friends? Well of course they needed a place of their own. There were four of them.

So, I took on the project of helping them out. I helped them get their own place. I showed them around the town on the buses. I directed them to the welfare office, they were new in town. I even helped feeding them one time. Gave her diapers and the like. I didn't mind helping out. They needed help and they had kids. I even helped them getting rides to the Kingdom Hall of Jehovah's Witnesses. Let's call the couple Ozzie and Harriot. They were party people and they made friends quick. They loved playing cards. So, they had people over all the time. I got them an apartment in the next street over from my apartment. We became friends. But that's not the screw up. The young man who visited the couple every morning was the screw up of my life.

Every morning I saw him walk over to Ozzie and Harriot's apartment. He lived across the street on the other side of me. I used to think how funny he looks. Tight shorts on and the same shorts every day. What a funny young man I would think.

One day I met him at Ozzie and Harriot house. His name was Dale. Funny young man I thought with the tight shorts.

Anyway, Ozzie and Harriot had a party. All their new friends were there. It was a big turnout. Dale was there also. My son and I were there too. This was actually the first time I had a good look at Dale. Never thought much about him.

My son was not yet walking but he crawled around. Ozzie and Harriot lived on the second floor and they had a balcony. I was very cautious about my son crawling around. Naturally right? Dale took the initiative to watch out for my son. I thought that's nice of him.

There was some other guy who didn't think I should give my son all the attention I gave him. He said some unkind things about my ways of mothering my son. Like it was a bad thing to watch and make sure he kept safe. What nerve of him I thought.

Then Dale said something and came to my defense. I thought that was kind of him to take up for me and my son. So how did I screw up my life? This party was the beginning of that screw-up. I got to know Dale.

CHAPTER 30

What do you want?

Why am I starting out with that question? Well that funny man that visited Ozzie and Harriot everyday took it upon himself to visit me. So, what do you want? Yes, I remember him from watching him every morning walking over to Ozzie and Harriot house. I also remember him from the party. He defended me. Remember there was a guy who talked bad about all the attention I gave to my seven month old son. As if I should let him run loose on Ozzie and Harriots' balcony that led to stairs on the second floor. Yes, I remembered Dale well. So, what does he want?

He obviously found out where I lived from Ozzie and Harriot. So, one day there he was at the bottom of my staircase at my apartment complex. The same tight shorts on.

I told him right away I was not interested in getting involved with a worldly man. I was trying to be a Christian and will only talk to men in the organization. I was not interested at all in him. Well, he came to his own defense saying that he was a spiritual person too. What kind he didn't say. Anyway, the conversation ended, and he went away.

But that was not the end of that funny looking, tight wearing shorts man. He proceeded to knock on my door on another occasion.

What do you want? Nobody is going to interrupt the peaceful schedule I have with my son. And besides, men are dogs, or so I presumed.

He proceeded to ask me if he could borrow something. I lent him the item and he left. He did it again and again. Borrowing items on different days of the week. I gave him each item and he would thank me and leave.

Then one evening he came over and asked me if I had any ice cream. This time Dale was dressed up. I said yes, come in. I gave him ice cream. Wow he won't give up, I thought. He ate the ice cream and we talked. He had a lot to say.

He was interesting, especially since he claimed to be a spiritual man. The first I ever heard that. I told him I was studying the Bible with the Jehovah's Witnesses. I told him about some of the teachings of the witnesses. Then he left.

He came back another time all dressed up. So, I let him in again. That was my Big Mistake!!!!! He wanted to borrow something again. I believe I gave him something to eat. That wasn't the mistake. The mistake was he kissed me and instead of kicking him out I allowed him to kiss me again. That was the hottest kiss I ever experienced. No one has ever kissed me like that. There was nothing more to do but go for it. Well needless to say I slept with him – another Big mistake!!!!! It was too hot to turn down. Whether I wanted it or not, a relationship was started.

His intellect was amazing. I wanted him to study the Bible and he agreed to study. So, we studied together. He told me his beliefs and I told him mines. Sounds good, right? WRONG!!!!!! We became lovers right away. It was easy since he lived across the street from me.

It was very important to me that he treated my son well. He was very kind to him. He would take pictures of my son. Then before I knew it, the time came for my son to take his first step. Dale happened to be there when he took his first step and Dale caught it on camera.

My son was very steady on his feet. I don't remember any falls. As a matter of fact, he took off running shortly after that first step. My son was 10 months old when he took his first step. It was a joyous day for me. Dale was there also cheering my son on. Sounds good right, WRONG!!!!

CHAPTER 31

Dale and I couldn't keep our hands off each other. I say this was a problem, but you are probably wondering why. After all, we got along, my son liked him, he was kind to my son, the sex is more than great; so, what's the problem?

Well first of all, this relationship was hot from the beginning. We could not keep our hands to ourselves. I don't mean to turn anybody on, but that was what it was.

We talked, we had spiritual discussions, we played with my son, I cooked for us, all as if we were family. Sounds good, right? Wrong!

I actually thought I was falling in love with Dale. Well how did he respond? He tells me, "I don't fall in love."

WHAT? You are in my bed at this moment, making love to me and you are not falling for me? I should have kicked him out then and there. Especially since my studies of the Bible warned me about the end results of such behavior.

I did not kick him out. I tried to look deeper into the situation. I had never heard such a thing and figured that this only happens in California. How can someone display such affection for the opposite sex and not fall in love? We got along, we tried to respect each other, we spent all our time with each other. What do you mean you, "don't fall in love?"

His explanation was not clear. As a matter of fact, it led me to believe he was just protecting himself. So, with that in mind, I thought I would do the same things and not fall in love with him.

Day after day, night after night we are together.

When it comes time for my studies, I kept them up. As a matter of fact, he sat in on one of my study groups. My bible study teacher didn't comment much about him. She treated it as if it was my own affair. I appreciated her attitude about my new friend.

Day in and day out we were together not falling in love. Soon my son turned one year old and I thought it was time for me to go back to work.

CHAPTER 32

What a change for me. I didn't work while I was pregnant. I had finished the Business College, but I couldn't get a job with my big stomach. That meant I had not worked for the two years when I was on welfare.

I was done with that nightmare, although I wouldn't trade the experience in for anything. I had a nice place to live, enough food to eat. The bills were paid. All I had to pay for were gas and electric and phone. Not to mention the fact that I had built such a close bond with my son.

I had to find a babysitter for my son. I knew that was going to be a problem since I had no family to help. What was I going to do?

I decided that the best thing to do was to ask around at the Kingdom Hall of Jehovah's Witnesses. I went to the Sunday meetings with my son. The people were nice to us and why not talk to someone about my problem - I needed a babysitter for my son. By this time, I had a job to go to. I was going back to the Mansion Inn hotel not far from where we lived in downtown Sacramento.

Sure enough, one of the baptized Witnesses knew someone that might be able to help. The potential babysitter was a bible study person of my friend. I thought this was great. My baby would be watched by someone who attended meetings just like me. Right away I started to trust that my luck had turned around. This was good, right? WRONG!

I arranged for this babysitter but would later find out that the lady from my Bible study group didn't really know the babysitter all that well.

At this time my main means of transportation was a bicycle that I rode all around town. My son would ride in a seat on the back of the bike.

I would drop my son off at the babysitter's home, she didn't live too far from me, and then I would go to work. My shift was 8 am to 4 pm. I worked mostly during the week but had some weekend hours as well.

Anyway, everything seemed to be going along just fine. Then one day I was dropping my son off and he started screaming to the top of his lungs. I had no idea what was wrong. I assumed that he was missing me, so I dropped him off and went to work.

That night I got ready for the meeting at the Kingdom Hall with my son. When I changed his diaper, he had marks on his behind. I was terrified and angry. Who told this babysitter to beat my son?! He was a good boy, no problem at all.

The next day I went to the babysitter's house and told her off. That was the end of that! Her explanation was she was trying to potty train him. Well I told her in no uncertain terms that I never said she could beat my son.

As it turned out, she was a very bad person with a lot of deception in her. She had lied about her personal life. She studied the bible but lied a lot to her bible study teacher. This information came out after my son's incident. If I would have known what type of person she really was, I never would have left my son in her care.

So, what do I do now?

While I was on welfare, I did a little babysitting for some people in the neighborhood who worked. I knew that there was a lady across the street from me with two small children because I sat for her every now and then. They were Mexican and spoke just a little English. The mother became a friend to me.

As it happened, my neighbor's sister-in-law was coming from Mexico. She was pregnant and wanted to work a little before her baby was born. Even though she spoke no English, she agreed to babysit my son. I didn't care about how she spoke, so long as she took good care of my son.

In the end she was a great babysitter. My son may have been too young to be talking at the time but soon he was understanding the Spanish language. I thought that was great.

CHAPTER 33

As time went on, I was still messing around with Dale, but I also kept up with my studies of the Bible. The more I studied the more I wanted to become a Jehovah's Witness. But how was I supposed to do that when I had this man that I was sleeping with in my life?

My son was walking and getting big. I wanted a good life for the both of us. Dale was consistent in his visits and I had a battle going on within myself. I wanted to keep growing spiritually in the Jehovah's Witnesses organization, but I also was drawn to Dale. I knew that I was going to have to eventually make a choice.

You see in the Bible my kind of conduct was a serious sin. If you do not know what sin is, it is the kind of behaviors you just do not engage in; it is absolutely not tolerated after baptism. It means your life, if you engage in some serious sins.

Now we all sin, we cannot help it. We are imperfect. But what I was doing, having sex without the benefit of marriage, well that's a big "no no" in the Bible. As long as I engaged in premarital sex acts, there is no way I could get baptized and become a Jehovah's Witness. You see Jehovah's Witnesses take the Bible literality. Whatever the Bible says, they will try to do it. No matter what they must give up.

As time went on, things were actually pretty good. My son was now over one year old, and his babysitters were very good people. I had a sense of wellbeing. There was a calmness about me. I finally thought I knew who I was and where I was going. Then one day, the State of California announced that they were building a low-income apartment building for families and persons that qualified.

Right away I applied for an apartment. They were building two- and three-bedroom apartments, not far from where I lived at that time. Great!

What's even better was that even before I was accepted for an apartment, I decided to dump Dale.

Dale was a distraction. Remember, he told me to my face that he didn't fall in love with anyone. So why did he keep coming over? We all know the answer to that. Well, I figured I better not let myself fall in love with him. It turned into a relationship about nothing more than sex. I wanted more from someone. I wanted to be a Jehovah's Witness first and foremost. My dealings with him were holding me back. He was interesting, but not that interesting.

I dumped him and was happy to do so. My son was very important to me and I wanted him to have a stress-free childhood. If I'm not happy than he would feel it. Dale was a waste of my time. It was a good move for me. I big load was off me as well.

Just me and you babe. I was totally happy again. No unnecessary distraction. My studies improved and I drew closer to my God Jehovah. Then one day it happened. It was time to move into the low-income apartment. I hate to brag, but I was like number five on the waiting list. When the day came to pick out which apartment I wanted, oh happy day. I picked a very nice two-bedroom apartment.

I was so happy with my life. My son was happy also. Then one day it was time to move in. Some very nice young men from the Kingdom Hall of Jehovah's Witnesses came and helped me move. They were so nice about it. My Bible study teacher set it up for me. That was so nice. And the apartment was so nice too. Everything was brand new!

My son slept the whole time we were moving. It was nap time for him. The next day when we woke up in our new apartment, my son was so happy. He couldn't talk yet, but he ran back and forth in the small hallway. That's how he showed me he liked the new place.

Things went well for us. By the time I moved in I was baptized into Kingdom Hall of Jehovah's Witnesses. I was so happy. It didn't bother me that I had to get up at five o'clock in the morning to catch a bus at 6:30, then drop my son off at sitters in order to take the bus back to the downtown area for work at 8:00. I was independent and a single parent. I worked for the two of us. Life was good.

My son and I got off the bus on the corner where we lived at about 5:30 every evening. We ate and were in the bed by 7:30. We got up the next morning again at 5:00. This was our routine. We attended two Jehovah's Witnesses meetings each week, one always on Sunday. I did not work on Sundays. What a schedule.

I was enjoying my life. Then one day, Dale was at the bus stop. He claimed he was just walking by. My son and I were getting off the bus and there he was. You see, I never told him what apartment I moved into. He knew what complex but that was all.

I was shocked to see him. I quickly told him I was not interested in being his friend. I had dismissed myself from him. He walked off and pretended that it was a coincidence, him being there when I got off the bus.

With so much going right in my life, what went wrong? HIM!!!!!

CHAPTER 34

I must tell my readers what happened before I moved to the new apartment. You see I was lying in bed in the old apartment after Dale left and it hit me all at once. Mind you, by now I was baptized as a Jehovah's Witness. I had allowed this man into my bed, after baptism. "What are you doing? What are you doing?"

I knew my next step was to repent, so I did in prayer. Next, I went to the elders at the Kingdom Hall. These brothers in the organization met with me as a group to help me with my problem. I told them what I was doing after baptism, messing around with my ex-boyfriend.

I was crying and everything. I was sorry for my actions. I had been baptized and knew that the organization had to protect the other members from persons who, like me, had committed a big sin against Jehovah. I was not ignorant of what I had done. I knew the consequences of my actions. I needed to be removed from the Congregation of Jehovah's Witnesses. I cried because I knew no one would talk to me.

I had made a lot of trustworthy friends while I was associated with the Congregation. I cried so much, because I was sorry for my actions right after baptism. I needed to be disciplined, and the elders did discipline me. They announced that I was on reproof at the next mid-day meeting.

This meant that I needed help from the Congregation members. I had not been disfellowshipped, meaning the whole Congregation could still talk to me. The members of the Congregation continued to talk to me, with caution. They knew I did something wrong, but it was up to me if I wanted to tell anyone what I did.

My new friends were leery of me because I was freshly baptized and screwed up somehow. To make long story short, Jehovah had mercy on me, and the elders did not disfellowshipped me.

You would think I would shape up after that ordeal, well I didn't. Shortly after the time Dale "coincidently" ran into my son and I at the bus stop, someone told Dale which apartment I had moved into. It didn't take long until he started knocking at my door.

After a while, I broke down and one night I let him in. That was a big mistake. I ended up sleeping with him again. This time when I went to the Elders, I was disfellowshipped. No one was allowed to talk to me for four months. It was terrible. I lost all my trustworthy friends.

I was determined to return to the Congregation after being disfellowshipped. I didn't miss a single meeting and I studied for each meeting. Finally, after four long months the elders reinstated me. No friends for four months. It was hard discipline to swallow. But it made me determined to straighten out my life.

I was determined to be a Jehovah's Witness again. It was up to me and I knew I needed the discipline.

You would think that this was the end of Dale. No…. He actually proposed to me. Young fool that I was, I accepted, even knowing that I was going to be unevenly yoked. I took that challenged and reasoned at least if I'm married, I won't get disfellowshipped again.

I think I actually loved him in large part because he was so determined to be in my life. Was that a good enough reason to marry someone? No, it wasn't. But I was young and dumb!

CHAPTER 35

I really thought I was doing the right thing, marrying Dale. I never thought he would ask me, but he did. What about love? Well I figured he would love me in time.

Time had passed and my son was now three years old when I married Dale. Dale was a kind person in a lot of his ways. It is hard to explain our relationship, it was different.

Dale was more like a brother to me, rather than a husband. It was weird, but I went along with it. No sweat off my back. After all, he was good to my son.

One thing that was odd was that he didn't want me to meet his parents, my in-laws. Dale's parents lived in Sacramento and Dale had told his parents we were living together. This was so strange.

But one day I had had enough, so I called my mother-in-law and said we had to talk. We met and I told her the truth, that Dale and I were married. Dale was strange, indeed.

Before I knew it, we were married for a year. Soon after our one-year anniversary, I became pregnant. After getting over the morning sickness, it was a good pregnancy, meaning I had no physical or mental problems.

Dale and I went thru the La Mas classes together with my son right there sitting in on the classes. Dale turned out to be an excellent coach.

When the time came, I made the mistake of calling my mother-in-law and I told her I was headed for the hospital. Well, she got there not too long after we arrived.

It was twelve hours of hard labor. My Mother-in-law kept telling me to scream. Each time she said that, Dale would whisper, "pay her no attention." I was determined not to give her a show.

What really upset me about my mother-in-law was that she bought a girlfriend to my birthing business. Now this person was a nurse, but who cares. I had never seen this person before and here she is in the middle of my giving birth to my daughter. My father-in-law was out of town at the time, so I guess she figured her nurse friend was the next best thing.

Finally, my daughter was coming. Unfortunately, the doctor who delivered my son couldn't deliver my daughter. This was a real bummer since I really loved my doctor.

All of a sudden it was picture time! This nurse friend of my mother-in-law started taking pictures. Now I actually wanted pictures, but I kept telling her to take them from the side. She was totally into what she was doing and completely ignored my request. Before I knew it, she was taking pictures front and center as my daughter was being born. Oh, was I mad. But as soon as my daughter was born, I could care less!!!!

Before I knew it, we were home with our brand-new baby daughter. She was seven pounds exactly and 19 inches long. She was beautiful. My son was exhausted because he had been with me in the birthing room for the whole time.

Tired or not, we were all home together, it was great. By then my son was four years old. As it turns out, he was never jealous of his sister. I'm pretty sure it was because he was very much included in the whole nine months of waiting for her to be born.

CHAPTER 36

To tell the truth, this so-called marriage was doomed from the beginning. The only reason Dale was still in the house was because I had his child. As I said before, we were more like brother and sister. There was absolutely no romance at all. Granted we did get along. That was because I wasn't trying to change him, and he wasn't trying to change me. Roommates with benefits. Sex, if he initiated. You might think that it was a good start and I have to say, it wasn't bad at first.

I was getting adjusted to him the first year of the marriage. I was taking him as the person he presented himself to be. He was a home body with a lot of dreams. I don't quite understand how someone who stayed indoors most of the time could accomplish his dreams. Me, I just wanted the bills paid. Between the both of us they were so I didn't have much to complain about. I'm not the nagging type anyway. Then bam, the baby was born, and the changes began.

I can list the changes he put me thru, with his actions and his mouth, but I won't dog him out. He is dead now so he can't defend himself. But I will tell you this and leave it to your imagination. After the birth of my daughter, Dale announced to me that he is not my husband. Straight out, he said, "I'm nobody's husband."

You can imagine my reaction. I'm thinking, "What are you talking? I got papers on you." Granted he did other strange things, but the strangest thing was him saying he was not my husband. Did we not go to Reno and get married? Yes, we did. The bottom line is that he hated me having papers on him. Even so, we didn't fight about it.

When my daughter was six months old, we all went on an airplane trip together to be with my family in Alabama. Dale was all for it. The occasion was a surprise anniversary party for my parents. It was their 40th wedding anniversary. This party took place in Fairfield, Alabama.

Of course, we were the highlight of the party because we had traveled the furthest, not to mention the fact that no one had yet seen my daughter. The party took place at my Aunt's house in Fairfield.

They had to tell my parents a little white lie to get them to show up at my mother's sister's house. My parents lived three hours away from Fairfield so one of my siblings said she would be visiting our Aunt in Fairfield and could my parents pick her up there. At the time my sibling lived in Maryland. This was no problem for my parents, they loved visiting the relatives in Fairfield.

About 40 of us were in my Aunt's house, just as quiet as we could be. Here they come. "Surprise!" Dale, the kids, and I stayed out of sight, and then we made our grand entrance.

It was a double surprise for my parents. Oh, everybody was screaming with happiness. My parents were very happy. There was so much southern hospitality. We had lots of fun and there was so much to eat. Delicious southern cooked food. Everybody was snapping pictures of everybody. We all knew that the next few days would be lots of family, fun, fun, fun.

I freely admit that my family is very unique. When my uncles and aunt were alive, they were a real team. It did not take long for Dale to see this family unity. The first night in my Aunt's house, Dale made love to me like he was truly in love with me. I could not believe it. He was acting like he was in love.

At least that is what I thought. You see Dale's family was from Sacramento, born and raised - aunts, uncles, cousins, and grandmothers. They were the complete opposite of my family. As a matter of fact, I didn't actually know most of his family, just his parents and his two grandmothers. The rest I didn't know or see unless it was at a funeral after someone passed away. In other words, they were not close as a family. At least not in my day.

Dale only had one week off from work, so after our brief stay in Fairfield, we went to the country, in Whatley, Alabama, to stay with my parents. Dale was finally acting like a husband and I saw another side to him. We had fun in the country, we even went to Selma, to visit my father's uncle. He lived so far back in the woods Dale was greatly astonished. He had never seen the likes of rural Alabama before. He was really enjoying himself and me too.

Then the time came for Dale to go back to Sacramento and go to work. We got him to the airport and away he went. I stayed a little longer. I just didn't want to come and go, for I never knew when I was coming back to visit.

We had a nice family visit. My son remembers the trip, but his sister doesn't, she was just a baby.

Back to Sacramento we had to go. I kept wondering how Dale was going to treat me once we were back home. Was he going to love me in Sacramento? Keep reading, but I'll give you a hint. After meeting my family, and understanding me better, and liking what he saw you would think that things would have gotten better.

CHAPTER 37

Well, it was two weeks that I was gone from Sacramento with the kids. Dale was gone one week. When he landed in Sacramento, or should I say tried to land in Sacramento, the region was covered in water. There was a terrible flood.

At first, they could not land the plane but when they did land, he said it was a sight to see - nothing but water everywhere. At least he got back home safe, even if it was during the 1986 flood in Sacramento.

Then it was my turn to say goodbye to my family. It was a bittersweet goodbye. I knew Dale had a good time in Alabama because of the way he treated me while we were there. Of course, I had a good time seeing everyone. The big question for me was do I have a husband when I get home?

Back in California things were back to what had become normal. He wasn't in love with me after all. How did I know? Well, Dale had strange ways to begin with. The things he did and said were strange. He would tell me that I was not "intellectually stimulating." My thought on that was, didn't you know that before you married me? I dismissed that comment about me anyway. He had no leg to stand on.

Perhaps the strangest thing was that he wanted a ménage a trois – a threesome. I told him one p____ in our bed was enough. Those things were just way too weird in my book. After that I didn't pay him much attention.

Then he started talking about how attractive he was to other women. Now wait a minute! I know men look at other women, but he shouldn't tell me about it.

This went on for much of my third year of marriage. I began to get jealous, even though I am not a jealous person. When we went out together, he made it a point to let me know how much he enjoyed checking out the woman that he found attractive. Oh boy, I could see it ending. As a matter of fact, he did this every time we went out. I was one jealous person. I didn't have to accuse him of wanting other women, he told me. What nerve!

I was determined to be a good Christian woman. Dale wasn't going to stop me from raising our children in my religion. After all, Dale made up his own religion and it was all about him. He was the King of narcissism. All he thought about all day was himself. By this time, the only thing we agreed on was that I would raise the kids to become Jehovah's Witnesses.

So, I took care of the house. I cooked and cleaned every day. I instilled Bible principals in our children every day. We even had recreation on a regular basis. Thankfully, the kids and I were gone a lot, doing spiritual activities.

Dale was not taken very seriously in our house, except when he out and out disrespected me. We did not fight in front of the kids. I'm sure they can count on one hand the times we fought in front of them.

When we did fight it was usually about other women and his attraction to them. He was a blunted fool. He saw no harm in his expressing his feelings about other women to me. Was I crazy for not wanting to hear about it? I think not. Yes, he was strange. But I was determined to have a Christian household regardless of his shenanigans.

If Dale wasn't working, he was always in the house, spending a lot of time developing what he thought would be his musical career. Dale considered himself to be an artist. He was dying to become famous one day. Dale played the base guitar, wrote music, and tried to sing. Oh well, who was I to say he wasn't going to be famous one day. This was a big part of Dale's life. He really wanted to become a well-paid artist.

CHAPTER 38

By this time, I had lost two siblings to death. Gail had been like a twin to me. She was the first person that visited me in Sacramento. Remember, she is the one who told that crazy boyfriend I was living with that if he hurt me, she would come back and kill him. More on Gail later in the book. First, I need to tell you about another one of my sisters, Lula.

After I moved to Sacramento, one of my siblings, Lula, kept up with me. She called me a lot, so I was pretty excited when she said she was coming to visit me. Lula had gotten to know Dale before she arrived in Sacramento in person. When Lula called for me, she and Dale would talk to each other on the phone. I was glad they hit it off.

Lula and her daughter, who was a few months older than my daughter, arrived at San Francisco Airport. It was much cheaper to fly into San Francisco than Sacramento.

I took them on a tour of San Francisco. We had lots of fun. We had the whole day to tour, and we did a lot of driving. The only problem was Lula was afraid to cross bridges. Well, she landed in the wrong city since San Francisco is on the tip of a peninsula with water on three sides.

She was very adamant about not going across the Golden Gate Bridge. She said there was nothing holding it up.

When we finally got back to Sacramento before it got dark, I knew we were going to have a good visit. Lula and I had become very close after Gail died.

Lula stayed for one week and during that week she went to a Congregation picnic with me, not to mention we went to the Kingdom Hall together. She enjoyed her stay. The week went by way too fast, but I knew that it was not going to be long before I would see her again. I had planned a vacation to New York City with the kids, something Lula knew before she came to Sacramento. In fact, Lula really wanted a California vacation.

After Lula left, it was my turn for a vacation so New York City here we come!

It was a fun vacation, but short and sweet. My Dad came up from Alabama and we had a ball. Lula was a lot of fun to be with and it was great to have someone I could pour my heart out to - talk, talk, talk.

I spent some time at one of my older sister's house too. She had a picnic for me and several of my old Jr. high school classmates came to visit. Two of my cousins came also, as well as an aunt by marriage. We had so much fun. There were even a couple of old friends from the neighborhood there too.

Then it was time to go back to Sacramento. My daughter was a year old and she flew for free, so long as she sat on my lap. All the way back I was wondering, "What was it going to be like with Dale this time?" I actually missed him a little.

He was there to pick us up but as we were approaching home, Dale said that he had something to tell me. "What is it Dale?" I asked. His answer, "I moved out." This hit me like a ton of bricks.

The conversation went something like this. "What the ......?! Why didn't you tell me earlier? I could have stayed in New York where my family could help me with the kids. Do you think I want to be a single parent with two young kids? Are you crazy?!"

Oh, I was so mad. I thought that Dale was nothing but a selfish pig. I told him to take his daughter and leave. Well, he left with his daughter and went straight to his mommy's house.

The next day when I got a hold of myself, I went to my in-laws' house. There he was in the bed with Mommy and my daughter. I was shocked.

I yelled, "Give me my child!" and took her back. After I left there, not much was spoken. Clearly, I was ticked.

CHAPTER 39

"Why? Why? Why?" I kept asking myself, "Why did Dale think I wanted to be separated?" When we met, I was a single mother of one and now I wasn't sure what would happen. In my mind, Dale was nothing short of a selfish pig.

While we were married, Dale was a bartender one block away from home. He worked in a family-oriented pub where his bosses really liked that fact that he was a family man, not to mention that they really liked me and adored our kids.

Dale always shared his tips with me, so if I wanted the money I had to go to the pub and pick up my share of his tip money. On one trip there I came face-to-face with at least one of the reasons for Dale leaving me.

There she was, sitting at the bar and looking like she owned my husband. She even had the nerve to smile at me. I got my money and left but every time I went there, she was sitting there talking to Dale. When I asked him about her, his only explanation was she was a friend.

Yes, she was the one. One day she smiled at me and said something that really set me off. I launched at her and Dale had to jump over the bar to protect her from me. I ended up scratching him and ripping his shirt off. Oh, it was on! No doubt she was the one.

This affair with her lasted about six months and she was always at his place of business or at his new apartment. We had about three confrontations during this time and each time Dale would get in the middle. She would tell me to divorce my husband. I really could have hurt her, but my baby was on my hip at the time. I really wanted to hurt her. Not because of Dale, he obviously wasn't worth it.

After six months of her he came back to me. I can't believe it, but I actually took him back. He told me how she was a freak from way back and that was the attraction. He told me all about her. For reasons I'm still not sure of, I forgave him, and we continued our life together.

By now I wanted to hurt him, so after taking him back I announced that I was taking the kids and moving out of California. At this point his daughter was almost two and Dale had adopted my son. Even so, he was really cool about my leaving with his children. Of course, all he would have had to do was ask me to stay. But he never did.

I researched places where we could move to. Utah had the least crime, so I thought about going there for a while. Then it hit me, why not move to Alabama and be close to family?

The closest town to my parents was Grove Hill, but I didn't want to live there. So, I found the nearest Kingdom Hall to my parents, which was in Jackson, Alabama, about 20 minutes from their home. I gave them a call and they sounded very nice. I did a little more research and determined that this was the right place.

There was a nice apartment complex in Jackson. The rent was cheap, so I called the apartment manager and told her my plans. She made it sound very inviting, so I sent her three months' rent. I figured it would take me at least three months to find a decent job.

By now I just wanted to get away from Dale, after all, he never asked me to stay. I finally accepted that this marriage was doomed from the beginning.

I didn't know how nice my things were until I sold them. Got good money for all the furniture. And then the day came for me to leave Sacramento. My best friend was backing me all the way. As a matter of fact, all my friends were backing me, even the ones that didn't know why I was leaving.

Dale and I slept together right up to the day I left. Finally, the children and I boarded the Greyhound bus heading to Alabama. We only had to change buses one time in Los Angeles, so we got the three seats in the back of the bus for the entire trip.

It took us almost four days to get there. What a trip! Dale had showed very little emotions about my leaving, so I did the same. We kissed and said goodbye. I left him to show him that he was not going to treat me like that and get away without even saying he was sorry.

CHAPTER 40

There we were on our way to Jackson, Alabama. There was a guy on the bus with us who was going a little further than we were. He was going somewhere in Florida. He was the most annoying person I met on a bus.

He must have thought he was some sort of gentleman. He took the liberty of looking after me and my kids. I get it, a young woman traveling with two small children. But that wasn't the annoying part. For all three days on that bus he would say in a loud voice, "El Paso, Texas." You see everyone wanted to know where you were headed. People were friendlier back then. But wait a minute, he was going to Florida. Why was he yelling El Paso Texas?

Because that's where he was from. I will never forget that guy, no matter how much I try.

Ma picked us up in Mobile at the bus depot and oh boy, was I glad to get off that bus. It was nice to see Ma again. Daddy was in the Veteran's Hospital in Montgomery at the time otherwise he would have been there to pick us up as well.

Jackson was about an hour and half drive from Mobile. When we got to Jackson, we went straight to the apartments where we were going to live. The people there were looking for our arrival.

I had three apartments to choose from. The one I chose was in the back. It was very nice, with no neighbors facing me and a view of plenty of grass. It was a two-bedroom, one-bath apartment and the bathroom was huge. There was even a washer and dryer hook up in it. Oh boy was I happy.

All the appliances were electric, and the power wasn't turned on yet. It was the middle of the afternoon, so we rushed over to the electric company to turn on the lights. I did not want to spend one night in my parent's house. That's how independent I was.

From there we went to Momma and Daddy's to get some beds they were not using. Much to my mother's surprise, Daddy was home from the hospital. We got the beds and left noting that Daddy wasn't in a very good mood. He had come home in an ambulance from the Veteran's hospital and was not happy.

It doesn't take much for Daddy to be in a bad mood. That's part of his make-up. I do not believe that Momma had a chance to tell Daddy that I was not planning on spending even one night at their house. I think that for a minute he thought I was going to move in. That certainly didn't help his mood.

On top of his concern for me moving in, I think he would have preferred for Momma to pick him up from the hospital instead of picking me up at the bus depot. I don't know if she was expecting him or not to arrive from the hospital. Whatever the reason, he was in a pretty bad mood, so we got the stuff I needed and left quickly.

On the way back to Jackson, I told my mother about my plans and where I was going to work. I told her that I had prepaid three months of rent. She asked where I was going to work so I told her about the Steak House just down the road from my new apartment. I would not need a car since I could walk over to the Steak House. It made sense to me.

We went back to the apartment and put the beds in the bedrooms. Momma gave me some linens too. I was expecting four big boxes from Sacramento, but they had not arrived as yet. Momma gave me a couple of chairs too. Momma had to get back home to Daddy, so she left before it got dark.

There was a Jehovah's Witness family living in an apartment near the office. They knew we were coming, so I walked over to their apartment and introduced myself to them. The family seemed nice enough. They were about the same age as me and had two small boys.

We didn't stay and the wife walked me and the kids back to our apartment. It seemed the right place to be at this time of my life. But then I started missing Dale.

I did not dwell on that fact that I missed Dale. My primary goal was to get a job. I already knew that I wanted to work in the Stake House. That made total sense to me. It was just down the road from my new apartment.

I knew I needed to feed the kids until I got work so I made arrangements for food stamps. With that out of the way, I started bugging the owner of the Stake House for a job, the waitress position in particular. You can believe me for a black lady in Jackson Alabama, in 1987 that was a pretty big-time job.

He didn't hire me at first, but I kept bugging him. I would take my kids up to the Stake House when it was at their slow time and sit them outside. Then I would tell the Stake House owner that I was a single mother and that my kids were right outside. I told him that I was living in the apartments at the end of the road and that I really needed a job. After three weeks of that he gave in and hired me.

Things were going well. The Jehovah's Witness family gave me and my kids a ride to the Kingdom Hall, and the wife and I became friends. Ma would visit and take me to the laundromat and grocery shopping. Things were good. Unfortunately, I was missing Dale.

My new friend saw I was missing my husband, so she let me call him long distance on her phone. Remember that family owned Restaurant and Bar he worked at, well they fired him after I left. They said that they didn't like him anymore. They could see what he had done to our sweet family. On top of that, it looked like he was going to lose his apartment too. Poor Dale!

CHAPTER 41

I got the job!!! What an accomplishment! I was the first black waitress ever at the Stake House. It was a big deal. In fact, it was the talk of the town. I didn't see what the big deal was, but you have to remember, this was Jackson, Alabama in 1987.

I worked mornings and some nights. I hired a teenager to babysit the kids at night. My mom helped with babysitting as well, and there was even a daycare center for my daughter. It wasn't long before I was able to buy a used car. The congregation helped out with furniture on a loan and I got my phone right away.

As soon as I got my phone, I called Dale. He told me that he was starving. I felt sorry for him. He told me that he would be down to see us as soon as he could. This sounded very nice, so I ran up my phone bill talking to him, trying to figure us out. I just couldn't figure it out.

Then it happened, my name came up for low income housing assistance since I was a single mother with two small children. My rent actually went down. I was so excited. That's how I was able to buy my car.

Sometimes I would take my daughter to my mom's home and sometimes I would take her to the daycare center. I usually started work at 11:00am. Sometimes I would do a split shift and sometimes I would work right through until 5:00pm. My teenage babysitter worked out very well for me. When I worked late, I would drive her home when I got off at 10:00pm and pay her out of my tip money.

Then my used car started breaking down. Finally, it needed a new engine, so I traded her in for a brand-new car. It was my very first new car and the payments were $199.99 a month. I was so happy because I could actually afford it thanks to my low rent and good job. Life was good.

There was one part of my life that was giving me some problem, my Jehovah's Witnesses friends. They seemed so weak to me. For the most part, they were gossipers. They talked about each other, and I am sure they had plenty to say about me. After all, I think I was the only single person with kids in the congregation. It is no wonder the congregation did not grow in size.

But I was doing well and didn't let their gossip stop me. I knew who and what I was supposed to be regardless of how other people acted. By now I felt that I knew myself and needed the spiritual food, that being part of Jehovah's Witnesses would bring.

CHAPTER 42

Well, time was passing by swiftly. I made friends with the white waitresses at the Stake House. They were all married with children, so they did not understand what it was like for me as a single mom. Little did they know it wasn't that bad.

Heck, I really enjoyed my job. The customers were great. It would slow down a little after the lunch rush, and on the days I worked to 5:00 we would have a few stragglers come in after the lunch rush. These were mostly guys who were working on the road. They would work a job in the area until it was over, then move on to another town to work. These men were regulars.

They were mostly white men, Southern Gents. They were very respectful. They would refer to me as "Mam." I didn't correct them because I loved the respect they showed.

I even became friends with some of these Southern Gents. During the slow times I would have only one or two customers so I would have nice conversations with these Southern Gents. I would talk and talk, and they were mostly good listeners. Some even talked back. What I really appreciated was they kept it professional. They didn't hit on me at all. It was the highlight of my working there.

It wasn't a totally great place to work. The boss was from Georgia and he was definitely prejudice. He would accuse me of things at work meetings that he knew were not true. Fortunately, I got along well with his wife when she would come to the restaurant. I Also got along well with his children.

He wasn't all that bad of a boss. He would let me have the two nights a week that the Jehovah's

Witnesses met. But still, I was the best waitress he had. I didn't steal food like one of the waitresses did.

The time for Dale to visit was rapidly approaching. I couldn't wait. I was so horny. Let's face it, no sex for almost a year is a long time. My waitress friends knew he was coming and what I was looking forward too. They asked me about birth control, and I told them I had been on the pill for about a month. They said, "Oh no, you better have a backup." They thought my pills might not have kicked in yet. Dale was due real soon, so I did what they said.

They were good friends and looked at my circumstances as pitiful. They did not want me to get pregnant. They had a hard time understanding how a man would let his wife and kids live across the country. You see Jackson, Alabama was a family town. People there did not get a divorce, at least not the most of them. Family staying together was a big deal.

CHAPTER 43

Finally, the day came for the children and me to pick up Dale at the Mobile airport. There I was in my brand-new car. It was a very small car, but it was new, and it was mine. We were looking good after a year of not seeing Dale.

I told the kids I wanted to surprise him about the car, so I asked them not to tell him about it. Well, why did I even bother? Daddy's little girl blurted it right inside the airport. "We got a new car!" Oh well, he could still see how well I was doing on our ride home.

Dale showed his ignorance by how surprised he was to see Mobile as a city like any other city. I don't know what he expected to see. He was surprised how nice it was.

The airport was an hour and a half ride to Jackson. Dale was also surprised to see how nice the apartments were. We ate and it was time to put the kids to bed. I was happy to see Dale and he was happy to see me. I really hoped that just maybe he would want to stay in this family-oriented State of Alabama.

The next day, we went to see my parents. So far so good with my relationship with Dale. I had plans for Dale.

I showed him our little corner of Alabama. We went to my place of business so my friends could meet him. We had a congregation picnic that we all attended, so the congregation met Dale. We even went to the Gulf Shores. It was the beautiful beaches of Alabama. The water was very blue at that particular time. My mother helped us with directions as I wasn't too sure of how to get there. We knew we wanted to return, and we did.

On another trip to the Gulf Shores that was just the two of us I introduced Dale to some musicians that performed there. Dale was very excited about this and seemed interested in playing music with them. It was a very nice trip.

Soon after that second trip to the Golf Shores I got the word that my grandmother in New York City was dying and was asking to see me. Ma and I packed up and drove there in my new car. I left Dale with the kids and a freezer full of food. I was planning only to be gone a week. Dale needed to be alone with kids anyway and I needed a break.

I figured it would take Ma and me at least 24 hours to drive to New York City. With a new car, I figured it would be no problem so off we went.

Momma knew the way to New York City without the help of a map. It was mapped out in her head; she knew every turn and highway by memory. It was amazing. We did not make one wrong turn or get lost.

I did all the driving because Momma didn't know how to drive a stick shift car and my car was a stick shift. We would pull into a rest stop along the highway for a couple of hours of sleep then kept driving.

We finally arrived in New York City and I was acting like a kid in a candy shop. This was still my home sweet home. We went straight to one of my sisters' house, then to another sister's house. Finally, we drove to the house of the sister where we were staying.

The next day we visited my grandmother in the nursing home. She was a little hysterical. She didn't like the nurses. I calmed her down and braided her hair. My mother and sister who came with me for the visit gave my grandmother, Nanny, Easter candy. The nurse saw it and took it away, Nanny was a diabetic. She had some of the candy anyway.

I whispered things in my grandmother's ear to keep her calm. Nanny had studied with the Jehovah's Witnesses before she went in the Nursing Home. We always had a good relationship, but the fact that she knew about Jehovah's Witnesses for two years made us closer.

After few days of visiting whoever I could we began our trip back to Alabama. The short visit did me a world of good. I had no problem taking the time off from work. I just simply told my boss that my dying grandmother in New York City wanted to see me.

We made it back to Alabama the same way we got to New York City with Momma giving directions and me behind the wheel.

CHAPTER 44

We got back to Alabama just in time. My daughter's hair was a total mess. It was all over her head and she was playing in the dirt out in front of the apartment. OH MY GOD!

When I checked the freezer, it was empty. Dale, no surprise, was looking pitiful as well. First thing I did was wash my daughter's hair and make a trip to the grocery store.

I heard from some of my neighbors that Dale had been jogging with the kids and having a good time in the open space we had. He did like to play, but Dale wasn't the smartest man I ever knew. He was actually surprised that Alabama had the same television programs as they had in Sacramento. He must have forgotten he was still in the United States.

Dale seemed to be enjoying his time in Alabama, even though he claimed right from the beginning that he was only staying for a month. "We shall see," was my thoughts.

I decided to quit my job. I wanted to start my own cleaning business and get back into selling Avon. I had left a real promising career in Avon when I left Sacramento.

I put an ad in the newspaper looking for jobs for the housekeeping business. My goal was to expand and eventually get big enough to hire people to do the actual cleaning.

Right away I got customers who wanted me to clean their homes. Dale and I would drop the kids off at Momma's and we would go and clean. I had already put in a two weeks' notice at the Stake House. The boss was shocked that I was leaving and said that I was his best waitress. This was a bit too late. I gave him a year of my life and he didn't seem to appreciate all my hard work.

We got enough cleaning work to live off, so long as I continued to sell Avon products. Then, to my surprise, Dale said he was heading back to Sacramento. How could he leave his family? During our time together in Alabama he and I did not have even one fight. We were actually sweet towards each other. I was very upset when he said that he didn't want to stay in "Bum F___ Alabama." I figured he just wasn't man enough to deal with being a true husband and provider.

CHAPTER 45

The day came to say goodbye and I drove him to the airport! I was really upset. Remember the hard times Dale had in Sacramento? I wondered how he would make it.

Well Dale made it back to Sacramento without problems. However, In a few days he called me and announce he was moving to San Francisco. He thought this was some sort of great career move. He said he would be able to make ends meet by having a roommate.

His new roommate was someone he had worked with before and they were both looking to make a career move. The big news was that Dale's "friend" roommate was a woman. "Friend, my you know what!" I told him. "Don't tell me your business, Dale," were my last words as I hung up the phone.

I didn't know it at the time, but something snapped inside of me at that very moment. Life became much more difficult for me. I struggled to take care of myself and the kids. I went from job to job. All these changes after he left put me in a terrible place.

One day I thought I couldn't' take it any longer. I took the kids, put them in the car, and just kept driving west. I got as far as Mississippi, but my mind had snapped. I broke into some stranger's house with my kids.

When he came home and found us in his house, he was really mad. As you would expect, he called the police and I got arrested. The authorities took my kids and put them in foster care. As for me, I went to jail.

I spent two days in jail before my Jehovah's Witnesses friends came all the way from Jackson,

Alabama, to get me out of jail. The man whose house I broke into dropped the charges, since it was pretty obvious that I had real mental problems.

Ma was away at the time, so Daddy went to the social services people and got the kids out of foster care. The Jehovah's Witnesses took me home, back to Jackson. The kids stayed in foster care for a week.

The next day Daddy returned from Mississippi and brought me the kids. I still wasn't right in the head. Daddy said I gave him a huge headache. I played Kingdom songs over and over. These were the songs we sang at the Kingdom Hall. This really did calm me down and I started to take care of the kids again. Unfortunately, this terrible time wasn't over yet.

A few months later I did an awful thing. I left the kids in the house alone. I took off and drove and drove, all the way to Mississippi. It pains me to remember this, but the kids were in the house alone for two days. My son took care of his sister as best he could for those two days. He couldn't cook so they didn't eat much. About all they had was peanut butter. I was told that Ma finally came and got them.

By the time I was well into Mississippi I got to the point I just couldn't move any more. I parked my car in front of some poor man's house and just sat there. The homeowner didn't know what to do so he called Sheriff.

The sheriff's deputy realized something was wrong with me, so he took me to the State Hospital, where I was admitted into the mental ward. By now, even I realized that I needed professional help. I was grateful for Ma and Daddy taking care of my children, but I knew I had to get better and take proper care of my kids.

The hospital was very nice. The doctors diagnosed me and were able to give me medicine to help me feel better. They told me I was going to have to stay on medicine for the rest of my life. Well, at least now I knew what was wrong with me. I made up my mind then and there that I was going to do whatever it took to do a good job raising my children. I was 32 years old, when I was diagnosed.

Everyone wanted me to get disability money through the SSI program. It looked like I wasn't going to be able to make a living any time soon. A big part of my breakdown was all the stress in my life. I had gone from job to job, and my cleaning business wasn't successful enough to support us. I had failed, at least that's what it felt like.

I spent three weeks in the hospital. Momma picked me up and took me home. I applied for SSI disability, but Alabama turned me down. I figured that California would take care of me, so I told my parents and made plans to go back to Sacramento.

Even before leaving Alabama, I got in touch with my spiritual Mom in Sacramento. She is the person that studied the Bible with me and helped me understand my religion.

I told her everything that was going on. My spiritual Mom was wonderful and agreed that I could stay with her until I found a place of my own.

One big question was how to get back to California. Driving seemed the best way so I called my husband and he agreed to come and get me.

Now I was back to getting rid of all my belongings. It was sad, but everything had to go.

CHAPTER 46

I vaguely remember staying with my step-grandma after one of my episodes. As a matter of fact, I stayed with her for several days after that episode. My mother was away, which meant that Daddy had the kids for several days.

In total I had three nervous breakdowns that year. I remember my step-grandma talking on the phone with Dale every day that I was at her house. He wanted to talk to me, but I refused to talk to him.

Then one day I got in my car and drove to Daddy's store in Whatley, Alabama. I picked up my kids and drove back to Jackson. Daddy was really mad at me; he didn't want me to take the kids. It was OK because I felt much better after venting all week with my step-grandma.

Anyway, I took the kids back, went home and acted like the mother that I knew I was supposed to be. I continued to take care of my kids and waited for Dale to arrive.

Ma got back in town, and we began planning my trip back to California. Ma thought it was an excellent idea for me to get on SSI. To tell the truth, I really had very little to say. It was as if I was coming out of a nightmare with limited options.

It was hard getting my brain back to normal. I was truly messed up mentally. But I knew that the most important thing for me was to finish raising my kids. So, I listened to the doctors and attended after-care programs for people like me. This wasn't all that easy since these sessions were all the way in Mobile. That was where the hospital was, making for a long drive three times each week.

It helped a lot to talk about my problem and listen to how other people were dealing with their problems. I came to terms with the fact that I had gone nuts for a while.

Mental illness has a very bad taste in most people's mouths, especially when I was growing up. Knowing that I was suffering mental illness was very hard for me.

If I was going to move, I had to get rid of a lot of my belongings. Boy, I accumulated a lot of stuff in a short time. I gave my mother a lot of my things. My step-grandma got a few things too. One of my neighbors got most of my kitchen things.

Then the day came for me to pick Dale up from the airport. I really didn't know what to think about him. I just needed help getting back to California.

I figured the move would be good for the kids. For one thing, school was a lot harder in Alabama then it had been in Sacramento. For instance, when we arrived in Alabama, the school wanted to make my son repeat the second grade. They said he was too far behind to begin third grade with the rest of the students.

I talked them into letting him stay in the third grade and you know what, he knew he had to catch up and he did. Boy, was that scary.

I still wasn't right in the head when Dale arrived. When he looked at me you could tell that he was a little scared. He really didn't know what to expect since I had refused to speak with him on the phone before he arrived.

Well, Dale had come and now we were going back to Sacramento. California here I come. My old landlords knew I was coming back. I couldn't believe it, but we had been gone for two years.

CHAPTER 47

Well, Dale was back in my life. At that particular time, I was only thinking about getting on SSI and finishing raising my kids. I really could care less about Dale. I had nothing to say to him. I didn't talk to him too much, and he got the message. My attitude was, "Let's get this over with."

Momma put new tires on the car, and I was very grateful for that. We had gas money, food money, and, of course, hotel money. Daddy came and picked up the washer and dryer that I bought. One of my friends moved into the complex so that she could help me. She was a big help with packing. She even took some of the kitchen stuff. Ma and my step-grandma got the furniture.

On the morning we were to leave, we arrived at Momma's house early in the morning to say goodbye. Momma said, "Leave the kids, Joan, at least until you get a place. Then you can send for them." That made sense, so that is what we did.

It was hard to say goodbye to my kids, but I knew they were in excellent hands. My parents always helped out with their grandchildren. I was not the only one in the family that needed help for their kids. I do believe everyone did, except for one sister. She never left her kids with my parents.

I truly understood that at this particular time I could use all the help I could get. The one thing that helped me the most actually came from Daddy. One morning he looked at me in my despair and said, "Joan, everybody gets sick one time or the other." You know, I never looked at it like that before. It sure eased my mind a bit. I wasn't feeling too good about myself, but I knew I couldn't dwell on it. I had to stay focused. I was going to finish raising my two kids.

After our goodbyes we left before sunrise. Dale and I drove and drove until the sunset. It was very quiet, since I had nothing to say to him. He did most of the driving.

We would stop at a hotel, and much to my surprise, he wanted sex with me. I didn't know how to feel, we were still married. So, I went along with it. I never thought anything would become of it anyway. "Why not?" I thought, things couldn't get any worse.

We drove and drove and finally arrived in Sacramento, California. I was glad to get out of that car. As I said, we didn't talk to each other on the way. I wasn't talking to anyone for that matter. I knew that I was going thru some kind of changes in my head and kept trying to figure things out.

It was the October when we arrived in Sacramento and there was a bit of a breeze. It wasn't cold, just a nice breeze. It was almost dark when we arrived at my spiritual mother's house.

She and her husband knew Dale and they extended us hospitality of staying with them for the night. The next morning, I drove him to the bus depot so he could go back to San Francisco. I didn't care if I ever saw him again.

The subject of his female roommate never came up during our entire trip across the country. I really didn't care; I was more focused on how I was going to take care of my children.

CHAPTER 48

The first thing I had to do was go to the welfare office and try to get some help. I applied for SSI, and now it was time to wait. The welfare office said that I have to have at least one of my children living with me in order to receive benefits.

Right away I called Momma and bought my son a one-way ticket to Sacramento. I had saved a little over $400 and his one-way ticket was exactly $400. Momma and Daddy put him on the plane, and he was on his way to me.

By then I had been in Sacramento for three weeks. I got approved for a one-bedroom apartment from my old landlords. What I really wanted was one of the low income apartments owned by the State of

California like I had left two years earlier. At the moment, I would take what I had to take.

I needed three bedrooms but could only get the one-bedroom apartment they were offering. When he arrived, my son spent one night with me at my spiritual Mom's house than we moved in the one-bedroom apartment.

It was a Friday evening and the electricity had not been turned on. We went without lights for the weekend, but I had an ice chest and we were able to keep some food in the chest. The gas was on, so I was able to cook for us.

I didn't care that it took me three weeks to get a place. All I could think was, "Give me my baby girl, Momma." So, when she heard I had a place, Momma made plans to get on the bus with my daughter, all the way from Alabama.

Fortunately, Momma was not taking the trip alone. Momma had a first cousin with children in Los Angeles, so they took the bus together, at least as far as Los Angeles. I was happy that Momma had a traveling companion.

By the time Momma got to Sacramento we had two beds in the bedroom, and a hide-away sofa bed in the living room. The apartment came with a kitchen table and some chairs. I received the other furniture from some of my Jehovah's Witness friends. My son was already in school and I had to get my daughter into kindergarten when she arrived. By the time Momma arrived it was November. Momma stayed and visited as long as she wanted.

My daughter could not go to the school down the street, the school that her brother was going to. There wasn't any more room, so I had to get her to a bus stop, and she got on a school bus and went to another school for kindergarten. No problem.

One Saturday I went to an Assembly. This is a spiritual meeting that lasted all day. I had to go to another town for this meeting. A friend of mine wanted me to go with him to the meeting. He was a gay Jehovah's Witness who did not practice that lifestyle, so no threat to my spirituality at all. This meant that I could hang out with him without the threat of doing some kind of sex act.

When I got back from the Assembly, much to my surprise, Dale was there. Momma had let him in. Wow, I was shocked. Believe it or not, I never even stopped to think about him for quite a while. I only dwelled on the kids.

Dale stayed for the whole week. I gave the bedroom to the kids and Momma. Dale and I slept on the hide a bed in the living room. I kept thinking, "When is he gonna leave?" He stayed from Monday until Friday. Meanwhile, Momma was getting ready to go back home to Alabama

Then the day came for Momma to go back to Alabama. I wanted her to stay longer, but she had to get back to Daddy. Dale had been staying with us every Monday through Friday morning. He worked only on the weekends in the Bay Area.

I still had not mentioned that female roommate to him. Then one day he volunteered that she had moved out. She told him that she couldn't take the competition of his wife.

By now it was obvious that we were back together officially. I told him in no uncertain terms, "If you ever cheat on me again, I am going to divorce you." He just looked at me and I walked away.

CHAPTER 49

Oh, I forgot to mention it, but I was accepted by the government to receive SSI. My children got benefits also, which was much to my surprise. I had enough money to pay my bills. That was a load off my mind.

After all the dust settled from the move, I became extremely depressed. I just couldn't kick it. Even so, I was not going to let my emotional problems get the best of me.

I felt horrible with four people in a tiny one-bedroom apartment. That situation did not help my mental situation at all. But I was determined to do all the things that I was required to do.

I got my days organized. My kids went to school. I went out in service on various days with my friends. Being in service meant that I was doing my door-to-door ministry. I didn't miss the meetings at Kingdom Hall. We met three times a week. I had to get the kids ready for the meetings. That was a big chore. But I was determined to continue on with my life, even though I felt like crape.

I never missed my therapist appointments. These meetings were really helpful. I was able to vent about my husband and get a bunch of stuff off my chest. Right away my therapist wanted me to get rid of Dale. I probably should have listened.

When I was at home with the kids, I was very depressed. I blamed it on the fact that we all shared one closet. That closet was a total mess.

Then one day after ten months in that awful one-bedroom apartment, there was a two-bedroom available in the same apartment complex I left almost three years ago. My spirits did lift up a little. Not to mention the rent was subsided.

Dale was supposed to help me move while the kids were in school. Big surprise, Dale showed up late that Monday after we were finished with the move. One of my friends from the Kingdom Hall came over to help me move. At least we got it done before the kids got out of school.

I gave the kids the two bedrooms and I slept in the living room. I was feeling a little better now that we had a bigger place.

While I was in Alabama, my in-laws moved out of Sacramento. They moved back to Sacramento shortly after I returned. The only reason I got along with my in-laws was because I treated them the way the Bible told me to treat them. It was a very good thing I had this understanding because if I had my way, I would not have treated them good at all. My mother-in-law was always trying to pick a fight with me, but I wouldn't give her the satisfaction.

We stayed in that two-bedroom apartment for almost a year, then a three-bedroom apartment came available. They gave the three-bedroom apartment to me and my family, so we moved again.

I still didn't feel comfortable enough with my husband to say we were going to make it. He continued to work in the Bay Area on the weekends. Fortunately, he made about the same money as if he was working full time in Sacramento.

We would even go on vacation together every year. One year we went to one of my family reunions. We packed up the kids and drove all the way to Birmingham, Alabama. The family that came from other States stayed in Hotels and boy did we have fun. The reunion lasted three days. Friday-Sunday. Each day was something different to do. A meet and greet, pool party, formal party, barbeque and some went to church together. It was a lot of fun.

Another thing that we did as a family was to go on family picnics in or around Sacramento. We always enjoyed the picnics together. One time I went camping with a good friend of mine. I needed a break from the family. My friend and I went way up into the mountains. We had fun, there was a big group of friends at the camping site. As a family we spent five days at Santa Cruz, CA. We also spent time in Florida as a family. So vacation was no stranger to us.

I finally decided to go back to work, but I wanted a job where I would be home when the kids came home from school. My first thought was to go back to selling Avon Products. This would be great. I could make my own hours, work while the kids are at school, and sell to my friends and neighbors. There had been a short time that I sold Avon before I had kids. I went for it.

Boy was I glad I got back in the business. I really enjoyed selling Avon, and I was a good Avon representative. Things were good for me.

CHAPTER 50

By this time, I had been married to Dale for thirteen years. I was getting comfortable in the marriage. It wasn't an ideal marriage, but we did get along. Then one day it happened, Dale cheated on me again.

This time I found a phone number. When I called the number, it turned out to be Dale's new roommate in San Francisco. Turns out that she wasn't sleeping with him, but he did have a girlfriend. The roommate gave me the girlfriend's number.

To make a long story short, I called the number and Dale was actually there, at her house. I explained to her that I was Dale's wife and she was shocked. Dale had told her that he was staying with his grandmother during the week in Sacramento.

I told her she can have him; I was going to divorce him. I assured her that I was not angry at her because she did not know about his family.

That was the last straw. I divorced Dale and was so glad to get him out of my life. I had hung in there much too long. It was like bricks had been removed from my shoulders. My son was now 16 and my daughter was 12. They had very little reaction to all of this madness.

I filed for divorce right away. I had to serve Dale with papers so a friend of mine took care of that, when Dale was in town. The kids met up with him at a restaurant and he bought his girlfriend so they could meet her. Although he started their relationship with a pack of lies, she kept him. Go figure.

My friend served him the papers and soon a court date was assigned for us. Dale never showed up for the court date. I was granted child support and the divorce. I was so happy to get rid of him. Although I never understood Dale, something was still not right. He just didn't seem to care about the divorce.

CHAPTER 51

It was time for a new life for me. I had to rehabilitate myself back to work force and now I wanted a full-time job. I enrolled in a program that helped get me ready to rejoin the work force.

At the end of the program I went on one job interview. They let me try out the job, and they hired me. I really liked that job. It was a new company, and I was getting in on the ground floor.

I just loved my new job. My boss was great. It was Monday through Friday, 7am to 3pm. These were perfect hours for me. I got home at the same time the kids did. It was very important to me to be there when they got home from school. I didn't work any holidays and I still got holiday pay. There were even benefits with this job.

One day, to my surprise, I got a child support check in the mail from Dale. I really wasn't focusing on when I was supposed to get a check, so this check helped out a lot. My rent was subsided and that was a big help too. Things were great; I was happy. I rewarded myself every Friday evening after work with a can of beer, and then I would do laundry. The days were flying by; it was just that kind of job.

One day my daughter got home before me, and she let my ex-husband Dale into the house. I had told her not to let him in when I was not home. Well, there he was, as if he never left. Laying on the carpet in the living room watching TV.

Dale explained that he wanted to babysit the kids. By this time my daughter was twelve and my son was sixteen, so my response was, "What the heck are you talking about? Get out of here." I really couldn't stand the sight of him. What he really wanted was to turn me into one of his girlfriends. The nerve of some people - nope, not today, not ever. Besides, the kids had told me that his new girlfriend was no looker. They said I looked way better than her.

Anyway, they would visit Dale from time to time in the Bay Area. I guess the girlfriend was acting like some sort of stepmom. To be honest, I had nothing against her. I just thought she was desperate. She had to be desperate, given all that lying he did to her. I don't know how she could have overlooked all that.

The time came that I wanted to visit Momma and Daddy by myself. Dale had no problem keeping my daughter while I was gone. After the divorce I gained some weight, but by the time I planned to visit my parents I had lost the weight and was back to a perfect size 12. One more time, Alabama, here I come!

I flew into Mobile. Momma and Daddy lived one hour and a half away from the airport. They wanted to pick me up from the airport, but I said, "No, I'm renting a car." That was actually exciting, knowing that I could take care of myself like this.

Momma and Daddy couldn't get over how well I looked. I stayed for a week. During the visit Daddy asked me what happened between Dale and me. I told him, "Daddy, he was nothing but a Casanova." Daddy rolled his eyes back in his head, as if he knew something I didn't know. As it turned out, Daddy did know something I didn't know. At the time, I did not comment on the look he gave me. I didn't want to discuss Dale. I just wanted to enjoy my special week with my parents.

Dale kept my daughter with him while I was gone. My son stayed home alone. I flew out of San Francisco Airport and didn't know any other way to get there and back from Sacramento. Since my son had his license to drive and I had a car, this was my best option. I really took a chance leaving him home alone, with my car. Fortunately, it all worked out.

When I landed back at San Francisco Airport, Dale was there with my daughter and his girlfriend, of all people. My son was also there with his best friend. I took one look at Dale, grabbed my daughter, and proceeded with my son out of the airport. I didn't even speak to Dale. I just couldn't stand that man.

One thing I saw while I was visiting Momma and Daddy was that Daddy's health was getting bad.

Daddy was on dialysis and I knew by the looks of things that Momma was going to need some help. I realized that soon I was going to have to move back to Alabama to help Momma with Daddy.

That meant I would have to leave that great job, and my great boss. At that time companies were generous with raises, if you deserved them. I was a good worker, and my boss rewarded me with good raises. I was going to miss that a lot. Well, Momma was going to need the help, so I started making plans.

I didn't move right away so I had to plan this carefully. After all, I had two kids to consider. It actually took about a year until I was ready to leave Sacramento. By then my son was 19 years old and working.

My son was going to need a place to live, so I collected everything he was going to need to live on his own. I cosigned for him to have his own apartment and watched my baby boy go out into the world. Fortunately, he had a very good job and was able to pay the rent.

I did not leave for Alabama right after he moved out. I waited to see how he would do on his own. Well, my son explained to me that he loved living in his own place and for the time I was still there in Sacramento, he did just fine.

By now my daughter was about to turn fifteen years old. As you might expect, she was more than a little upset with me when I told her we were moving back to Alabama. I knew it was not going to be a good move for her. She had lots of friends and she was doing home schooling by then. She had also been baptized as one of Jehovah's Witnesses. Baptism was totally her decision, but I didn't think she was ready to get baptized.

The time came to move, so I rented a big U-Haul truck. I decided to keep most of my things this time. My best friend and her friend helped me clean the apartment. It looked like it was like brand new, when we finished cleaning the apartment. Dale even showed up and gave me $700 for the move. Boy did that help a lot. By then I stopped hating him.

My job gave me a nice going away party. I had been on this job for four years by then. It was truly a bitter-sweet goodbye. I asked myself, "When was I going to get it right?" That's how I felt. My son was 19 at the time and when we first moved into that apartment complex, he was just one and a half. I really thought I was never going to see California again.

My son did most of the driving to Alabama. He got some time off from work. He was a cook in a very nice, famous restaurant called Morton's of Chicago.

CHAPTER 52

Well, I started working for the school district in Grove Hill, Alabama. I needed a job that was flexible because I had to drive Daddy to his doctor appointments in Mobile. The appointments were two times a month, not to mention Momma would leave and go out of town on a regular basis. That meant I had to take care of Daddy while she was gone.

The best job for me was substitute teaching. I would do all the grades. It really worked out good. I was on call and it seemed they always called me at the right time. Daddy had a lucrative business on the property so helping me with my car payment was no problem for him. On the way to Alabama I put my new car on the back of the U-Haul truck that my son drove.

I had a house to live in, rent free, I just paid the utilities. Soon Daddy quit paying the car notes on my car, so I managed to pick up the payments. I worked and sold Avon and was always there for Momma and Daddy.

My daughter was no picnic. I ended up sending her back to Sacramento for the 12th grade.

My daughter did home school in Sacramento, and she worked as a Nanny. When it was time for her to get her high school diploma, I made arrangements to go to Sacramento and surprise her. I planned to and bring her back to Alabama.

It was the end of December and she was ready to graduate. The work she did in school in Alabama helped her to get out of school in Sacramento's home school program a lot sooner.

I surprised my daughter while she was working. You could tell by the looks of things she was on her own. My son was still working at Morton's of Chicago. He managed to see me before I left with my daughter. He helped me ship her belongings back to Alabama.

I got to see my ex- in laws. My father in-law helped me with expenses on a loan. My daughter had not stayed with her grandparents. I didn't like her looks, meaning her dress and her hair were unruly, but she was in one piece. I was grateful for the friend that did look after her.

We flew back to Alabama on Christmas Day. Meanwhile back in Alabama, Daddy started to get sicker. He was tired of going to the clinic and doing his dialysis. So, his doctor told him he can do home dialysis.

This meant me and Momma and Daddy would have to be trained how to do the home dialysis This also meant Daddy had to have an operation in order to do a home dialysis. The operation was in his abdomen.

Momma and I did his dialysis three times a day. Daddy never did it. Momma did it two times and I would do it once a day. But Momma would go out of the town and I took full responsibility of Daddy.

On average, I would cook for Daddy once a week, but when Momma was gone it was three times a day.

Daddy was a grump. But that was overlooked because we treated him like the king of the household that he was.

Daddy spent five years on dialysis and then he passed away. Daddy was a big man in Whatley, Alabama. He was a self-made millionaire when he died. But before he died, he shipped my daughter off to stay with her Aunt in Denver. There was nothing for her to do in Whatley but to get into trouble. He was not having it.

CHAPTER 53

It was kind of unbelievable that three years had gone by since I left Sacramento for the second time. It didn't take long for me to realize that I was a city girl from New York City and was not ready to rock on the front porch, so to speak, in the country.

When I left Sacramento for the second time, I thought that I wanted a slow and boring life. I was wrong. Well what to do.

I had a friend in Atlanta, Georgia. Someone that I knew from way back in Sacramento. I thought that I needed a vacation. Daddy was gone and when his funeral was over, I had this overwhelming feeling of wanting to get away for a while. I called my friend and went to visit her. Atlanta, here I come!!

I stayed with my friend for a week. Atlanta was exciting. She showed me a good time. Of course, we went to the Kingdom Hall. I enjoyed myself. We also did the night life. Nothing too risky. We went out to dance, basically we danced by ourselves. The men were not asking us to dance. A lot of people danced alone. The restaurants were yummy too. The week went by fast and I headed back to Whatley.

By then I was getting interested in health products. As a matter of fact, I introduced a health product to Daddy, and he felt 100 percent better. But the reason he stopped taking the health product was Momma cooked him some oysters for dinner. I saw on the news that day in my house not to eat oysters. I ran over to Momma and told her what they said about oysters on the news that day. Not to eat them. Well it was too late. She already gave them to Daddy. That very day he was sick. Even though he had been taking the health product that I gave him for some time, he blamed the health product got him sick. No Daddy it was the oysters. But he wouldn't listen he stop taking the health product. Even though he started walking better and driving his truck again. I was sure Daddy would have lived longer if he kept taking the health product. He had overall better health.

I started getting restless. Nothing to do but work and go to the meetings. No social life. I know, I'll move to Atlanta GA. It won't be too far from Momma. A six-hour drive. So, I started making plans to move to Atlanta. I wasn't hanging up my shoes yet.

I stayed with my friend and her family for one month than I took the apartment across the hall from her. It was a cute one-bedroom.

I really liked Atlanta. It was different from Alabama in the way that it was sophisticated. Lots to do and see in Atlanta.

I landed a good job that lasted five months. But before that I worked in a Mall for a very short time. I could tell the job was not going to last.

The job that I had for five months was supposed to be a temporary job for six weeks. It was in a cancer clinic. Lots of work to be done. I worked in the medical records department.

Then one day they asked me what I did on the weekends in the break room. I told them. I went door to door with the Jehovah's Witnesses, I was one. Well, right after that they called me in and told me there was no more work. Liars. I had forgotten that my friend that worked there too told me at the beginning of the job not to tell them she was a Jehovah's Witness.

Anyway, I lost that good job. I knew they were about to put me on permanent. After that good job was gone, I went from job to job. A total of seven jobs in one year. I was stressed. The reason for that was because in 2005 they did not have job security in Atlanta GA, if they did not like you, they let you go. I only quit one of the jobs that I had. I liked Atlanta but Atlanta didn't like me.

My good friend told me to come back to Sacramento. It was too stressful in Georgia. I hated to leave but I couldn't go on like that anymore.

Not only was I leaving for better economic reasons, my son joined me within that year. I left him in Atlanta and within that year he got married to a girl.

He wanted me to tell him what I thought on the way to the courthouse to get married. Well, that was a decision he was going to have to make on his own. Although I knew he didn't know her. His marriage lasted five years. Momma had to go!!!

CHAPTER 54

While I was away from Sacramento, Dale my ex-husband and I became good friends, or so I thought.

This time I told him I was moving back to Sacramento and I asked him if he could come to Atlanta and help me drive back. Right away he said, "No." I could do the drive on my own.

Three of my friends in Sacramento helped me out financially to make the trip back. This was a much-needed loan. At the time I was not working at all.

I gave my son a little wedding party after he left the courthouse with his new bride. Just the three of us were there.

A few days later I left on my own to drive back to Sacramento, a lone driver heading west. I stopped in Alabama to say goodbye to Momma. She was not happy about me driving all the way to California alone. Nor did she want me to go back to California at all. She thought this was too far from the family.

My son didn't want me to leave Georgia either, especially since he had a new bride.

I got in touch with my old job and they rehired me over the phone. There was a job waiting for me to arrive in Sacramento.

I took Interstate 10 from Mobile all the way west till I hit interstate 5 in Los Angeles. That was my route. I drove from sunup till sundown. I'd stop at a motel and sleep, then start all over the next day. It took me four days to get to my friend's house in Sacramento. After I arrived that afternoon, my job was expecting me to come in the very next day. I did show up tired, but in one piece.

Once again, my old landlords knew I was back in town, but this time with no children. The two kids of mine were now on their own. My son was in Atlanta and my daughter was in Denver, both on their own.

I stayed with my friend for three weeks and then moved to a studio apartment. Boy, I never thought I would live in a studio again. But it was mine and it was private. I lived there for almost a year, then I moved in with an elderly lady who needed some help.

She had a big house. I stayed with her for two weeks. She was not Jehovah Witness and she was crazy. I knew I had to get out of there quick.

Then I moved in with another friend of mine; she was single like me. We got along just fine. I stayed with her for three months, then my spiritual mother told me about these apartments in the Land Park area that were available. I went and checked them out.

CHAPTER 55

Oh my God, I fell in love with the apartments right away. They were huge. I figured that if I get in there I would not have to move again. It was a struggle to get in, but I am a persistent person. I will bug you to death till I get what I need.

One day the apartment I wanted opened up to me. I loved the apartment. As a matter of fact, I'm still living there today. I moved five times in one year in Sacramento before I landed this great one-bedroom apartment. I love it because it has a front door and a back door. It is more like a home than an apartment.

I was done moving, finally. My kids were in there 20's and we were all on our own. Yippie! Time for me to really live my life.

CHAPTER 56

Times were hard for me this time around in Sacramento. It was November of 2005 and the recession was hitting Sacramento hard. Although I had a job, I needed a second job to make ends meet. So, I worked a full-time and part-time job. There were no raises to get from your employer and rent was going up.

My life was full. Two jobs, the meetings at Kingdom Hall, eat and sleep. That went on for a while. I had no energy for anything else.

Then it happens, my daughter left Denver. I really don't want to get into what happened when she moved back to Sacramento. All I can say is she moved in with me and it wasn't pretty. The move-in lasted one year.

Goodbye daughter! Boy had she changed. Our relationship will be rocky for now on, but at least I was able to help her out.

My son was struggling with his wife in Atlanta. That was not a surprise. I don't want to get into that either.

Then I got a call, "Joan I'm moving to Los Angeles. I need you to pick up some of my things." It was Dale, my ex-husband. "What? I'm not coming to San Francisco to pick up your stuff." He kept on and on. He wouldn't take no for an answer.

I told him, "First of all, before you move to Los Angles, you need to come and see your parents in Sacramento." It had been five years since he saw them, and they were both in bad shape health wise. His response was, "No, please come to San Francisco to pick up some of my stuff. I'll come back to Northern California to see my parents real soon."

This went on for several days. I would tell him "No, you need to see your parents before you make that move." And he would say, "no." He had broken up with his girlfriend two years prior to this conversation, and I just didn't want to be alone with Dale ever again. But eventually I broke down. I took one of my girlfriends and headed out to see Dale in San Francisco.

CHAPTER 57

"OH MY GOD!" That was my feelings when I entered Dale's two-bedroom house by the beach in San Francisco. What the Hell? Dale looked a little disappointed that I brought a friend with me. But that's to say the least. His place in San Francisco was like reading the handwriting on the wall. I could tell there was no women coming in and out of that house, only men.

As a matter of fact, he always had men in the background when I would speak to him on the phone. We were friends now and spoke on the phone sometimes. What the heck was this? I looked at my friend, she could sense it also. Nothing but men been in this place.

Right away we had to go to the bathroom. We wouldn't even sit on the toilet. Then Dale took me into his second bedroom. It was all black. I yelled,

"What is this, a dope room?" "No," he tells me, "My roommate committed suicide in here."

I'm asking, "What do you want Dale?" He said something then we left that dark dismal room. I never saw the likes of it again. Dale had a few items he wanted me to take. The only item that was of value was a guitar and two gold lamps trimmed in 18 caret gold. He said I could sell the guitar and give the lamps to my daughter. Dale seemed very disappointed with the short visit. I told him to load the car and I left San Francisco.

The conversation in the car with my girlfriend was, "HE's GAY. No wonder my marriage didn't work out. He shouldn't marry any woman." OH MY GOD, everything finally fell in place. Up until now I had a big question mark as to what happened to my marriage. It was not the other woman. Now I knew that. Was I that blind? The wife is the last to know!

I can see clearly now. Dale obviously wanted to tell me something, about himself. And couldn't because

I had my friend with me, so the house where he resided spoke for itself. Two years after his girlfriend left. OH MY GOD! The veil was off! It makes sense now. What a relief. But what kind of head games was he playing with me? All kinds, meaning he had presented the fault in our marriage was mine. He said I wasn't his friend, and of course I was not intellectually stimulating. What a crock.

This attitude is typical with down low brothers. That's a term I got from one of Ophrah Winfrey's shows. Men that sleep with men and have wives, children, and girlfriends, but they do not claim to be gay. What a CROCK!! It was too late to address the divorce because it was over. I never mentioned it to him, that I knew he slept with men. Women were his cover up. My friend had never met Dale before, but yes, she picked up on it also.

Dale stayed in Los Angeles for two years before he made it back to Sacramento. It was about time, I thought. His parents were just barely holding on.

CHAPTER 58

Finally, after living in Los Angeles for two years, I was able to talk Dale into visiting his parents in Sacramento. They were both sick. I knew if Dale saw their condition he would move back and take care of them. After all, he was their only child.

Well the day came for his arrival. I was to pick him up at the train station in downtown Sacramento. I told him he could stay in my apartment since I was going on a trip to North Carolina to attend a college graduation. I also gave Dale access to my car since he had to drop me off at the airport and pick me up when I got back.

When I first saw him, I asked myself, "Is that Dale? It doesn't look like him. Oh, it really is him." I recognized the way he walked. Dale had changed so much in two years. He aged so much. When I saw him last in San Francisco he looked like himself, but when he got off that train, I did not recognize him at all in the face.

Dale and I went back to my apartment, and we stayed up all night talking. I needed to square things up, letting him know what-was-what with me. I told Dale I never wanted him from the beginning. I really always wanted Buck, my son's father. I didn't care about that girlfriend; I was just worried about the bodily fluids he was passing on.

I said something else but don't remember what it was. The point was to get these things off my chest. Funny, he had nothing to tell me about myself. You see, I was a good person and a good wife to him. Any man would have loved to have me.

Anyways, we talked about family, and we just caught up and I squared things with him. I never mentioned anything that happened to him after the divorce. It was none of my business. I just knew he was no threat to me as far as him trying to get me in the bed. He knew I knew about his lifestyle in San Francisco. It was obvious. He probably wanted to tell me about it when I went to San Francisco to pick up a few of his things. But because I had a friend with me there was nothing to be said.

Dale ended up moving back to Sacramento. His parents needed a caregiver, other than the ones helping out with his Mom. Dale lived with his parents for five months and then something tragic happened. Dale got out of the shower one day early in the morning and dropped dead on the spot. Dale had a diseased heart and had a massive heart attack.

Dale never went to see a Doctor, but he knew about his heart. I say that because during the 14 years we were married he never went to a doctor. He hated doctors' offices.

We found herbs for the heart in his belongings. Dale's death was the biggest shock I have ever had in my life. Dale was 51 years old and died in December of 2009, not too long after Michael Jacksons death. It seems that a lot of people born in 1958 died that year. Not that I look into things that pertains to that year, but I know it was a lousy year for me. I couldn't wait for it to end, and then when the year was almost over, Dale dropped dead. Dale came in this world naked and left it naked. Dale was a nudist. He would not have it any other way.

CHAPTER 59

For me, I'm in a good place right now. I learn something new each day. My God teaches me constantly. How to improve my life according to his will. I no longer do my will, but his. If I were to do my will, I would make a lot of mistakes. I would do bad. I have always done good when I follow God's rules. I no longer know what it is like to live my life doing my own will. And do not want to go back to that. It's important to me to live by God's standards.

Everyone is important to God. He is not partial to anyone. Not even the most important person in the world, according to Man's standards. The homeless people in the streets are not less of importance. But not to God, the homeless person is just as important as the most powerful person in the World to God. And if you think you are more important than someone else you miss the point that God is LOVE. God sees no difference in you or me, or he or she. God wants us to see things the way he does.

Everyone claims to have this or that kind of religion, but do you try to be like God and have LOVE for all mankind, regardless of any race, religion, or ethnic group? God welcomes all mankind to work and serve him forever. People recognize God's son, Jesus Christ, but will not say God's name, the one who sent forth Jesus Christ. It's in the Bible. His name is "Jehovah." Well, I got my sermon out of the way.

I just want to say before I wrap this book up, everyone has a book in him. It took me ten days to write this book, and that's just rounding off the time I spent writing it. It could have been less than ten days.

I can only hope I was able to give some kind of Witness to my God Jehovah.

I used my ex-husbands real name. He always wanted to be famous, if you read this book in a way he will be.

I feel it's important to warn all the up and coming ladies in the world. Use your head, don't widen your legs. You don't know who he's been with or who he's going to be with. He's not going to tell you. Think with your brain, not your heart, the heart will fool you. Your life depends on it. You ARE important to God.

Yes, we all have sexual urges, but is it worth your life? Desires will get you in so much trouble if you live by them. Wait till your married. It's a good tradition and a Godly rule.

Nothing is funny about a dead body. I don't care how they got that way. Death is an enemy, but some day death will be a thing of the past. All you people that believe in going to heaven can go already. The truth is no one wants to go. I believe in heaven, but I was born on earth, what's wrong with the earth besides all the bad things around us? The earth is beautiful. This is my home. And no man is going to fix it. Only GOD is going to fix.

Ladies keep your legs closed. I've experienced death in my family numerous times. Numerous people were murdered in my family. Diseases can murder you.

This rawness I have in me is not ugly. It is quick and to the point. Some people think my truth is painful because it is presented in a raw manor. Sorry,

I just can't pull your leg. I can't smile in your face and think of something different.

Sorry, I can't answer all your questions, it depends what you ask and your motive for wanting to know.

Nosy people make me ill. If I am going to be nosy, I will let you know I'm being nosy. I can't get mad at you if you cannot comply with my rawness I understand.

I can tell if a person likes me, so if you are being nosy and you are not a friend, I take offense.

You might know of me but that doesn't mean you know me. I'm not complicated. Maybe a little too honest. I never go out to deliberatively hurt someone. I'm not revengeful at all. I let my God Jehovah take up the revenges for me. I'm not perfect at all. But I am a good friend to those that seek to be my friend. I'll try to initiate friendship but will not pursue if not returned. That's ok, everybody is not for everybody. One day everyone will be friends and I can't wait for that kind of society. Sure, you say, well, read the BIBLE, it's in there. Marvelous future for all mankind. That's the Hope I have for you, you, and you.

ABOUT THE AUTHOR

Just Joan is a true story about a girl growing up in Hollis Queens NYC. Joan was a sibling to 9 persons. Joan's parents were married in 1946. The ten children were born in NYC. Joan was the first to be born in Hollis Queens, NYC. Joan was her parents 7th child to be born to this reunion.

Joan had a unique childhood. As child I was referred to as colored. Joan always and to this day acknowledges herself as a Black American person.

As a young person in the 5th grade Joan started her 1st book. But realizing I had a very limited number of things to write about Joan did not finish the book. Joan likes to write about things that truly happened to herself, or others that she grew up with.

Joan was first published in 1981. It was a letter to a magazine, The well known Ebony magazine published my letter to the editor.

Joan wrote an experience that she had at a class reunion in the summer of 2016. The local newspaper published that experience.

Joan is a very confident person that she will be published again by the AuthorHouse.

Lightning Source UK Ltd.
Milton Keynes UK
UKHW010633040920
369353UK00001B/106